DEPARTMENT OF THE TREASURY TECHNICAL EXPLANATION OF THE PROTOCOL SIGNED AT WASHINGTON ON JANUARY 14, 2013 AMENDING THE CONVENTION BETWEEN THE UNITED STATES OF AMERICA AND THE KINGDOM OF SPAIN FOR THE AVOIDANCE OF DOUBLE TAXATION AND THE PREVENTION OF FISCAL EVASION WITH RESPECT TO TAXES ON INCOME AND ITS PROTOCOL, WHICH FORMS AN INTEGRAL PART OF THE CONVENTION, SIGNED AT MADRID ON FEBRUARY 22, 1990

DEPARTMENT OF THE TREASURY TECHNICAL EXPLANATION OF THE PROTOCOL SIGNED AT WASHINGTON ON JANUARY 14, 2013 AMENDING THE CONVENTION BETWEEN THE UNITED STATES OF AMERICA AND THE KINGDOM OF SPAIN FOR THE AVOIDANCE OF DOUBLE TAXATION AND THE PREVENTION OF FISCAL EVASION WITH RESPECT TO TAXES ON INCOME AND ITS PROTOCOL, WHICH FORMS AN INTEGRAL PART OF THE CONVENTION, SIGNED AT MADRID ON FEBRUARY 22, 1990

This is a Technical Explanation of the Protocol signed at Washington on January 14, 2013, the related Memorandum of Understanding signed the same day, and a subsequent Exchange of Notes dated July 23, 2013 (hereinafter the "Protocol", "Memorandum of Understanding" and "Exchange of Notes" respectively), amending the Convention between the United States of America and the Kingdom of Spain for the avoidance of double taxation and the prevention of fiscal evasion with respect to taxes on income, signed at Madrid on February 22, 1990 (hereinafter the "existing Convention") and the Protocol, which forms an integral part of the existing Convention, signed at Washington on November 6, 2003 (hereinafter the "Protocol of 1990").

Negotiations took into account the U.S. Department of the Treasury's current tax treaty policy and the Treasury Department's Model Income Tax Convention, published on November 15, 2006 (the "U.S. Model"). Negotiations also took into account the Model Tax Convention on Income and on Capital, published by the Organisation for Economic Cooperation and Development (the "OECD Model"), and recent tax treaties concluded by both countries.

This Technical Explanation is an official guide to the Protocol, Memorandum of Understanding and Exchange of Notes. It explains policies behind particular provisions, as well as understandings reached during the negotiations with respect to the interpretation and application of the Protocol, Memorandum of Understanding and the Exchange of Notes.

References to the existing Convention are intended to put various provisions of the Protocol into context. The Technical Explanation does not, however, provide a complete comparison between the provisions of the existing Convention and the amendments made by the Protocol, Memorandum of Understanding and Exchange of Notes. The Technical Explanation is not intended to provide a complete guide to the existing Convention as amended by the Protocol, Memorandum of Understanding and Exchange of Notes. To the extent that the existing Convention and Protocol of 1990 have not been amended by the Protocol, Memorandum of Understanding and Exchange of Notes, the technical explanation of the existing Convention and the Protocol of 1990 remains the official explanation. References in this Technical Explanation to "he" or "his" should be read to mean "he or she" or "his or her." References to the "Code" are to the Internal Revenue Code of 1986, as amended. References to a "Treas. Reg." are to regulations issued by the Treasury Department.

Article I

Article I of the Protocol revises Article 1 (General Scope) of the existing Convention by deleting references to Article 20 of the existing Convention, by adding new paragraphs 5 and 6.

New Paragraph 5 of Article 1

New paragraph 5 relates to non-discrimination obligations of the Contracting States under the GATS. The provisions of paragraph 5 are an exception to the rule provided in paragraph 2 of Article 1 under which the Convention shall not restrict in any manner any benefit now or hereafter accorded by any other agreement between the Contracting States.

Subparagraph 5(a) provides that, unless the competent authorities determine that a taxation measure is not within the scope of the Convention, the national treatment obligations of the GATS shall not apply with respect to that measure. Further, any question arising as to the interpretation or application of the Convention, including in particular whether a measure is within the scope of the Convention, shall be considered only by the competent authorities of the Contracting States, and the procedures under the Convention exclusively shall apply to the dispute. Thus, paragraph 3 of Article XXII (Consultation) of the GATS may not be used to bring a dispute before the World Trade Organization unless the competent authorities of both Contracting States have determined that the relevant taxation measure is not within the scope of Article 25 (Non-Discrimination) of the Convention.

The term "measure" for these purposes is defined broadly in subparagraph 5(b). It would include a law, regulation, rule, procedure, decision, administrative action or any other similar provision or action.

New Paragraph 6 of Article 1

New paragraph 6 addresses special issues presented by the payment of items of income, profit or gain to entities that are either wholly or partly fiscally transparent, such as partnerships, estates and trusts. Because countries may take different views as to when an entity is wholly or partly fiscally transparent, the risk of both double taxation and double non-taxation is relatively high. The provision, and the corresponding requirements of the substantive rules of the other Articles of the Convention, should be read with two goals in mind. The intention of paragraph 6 is to eliminate a number of technical problems that could prevent investors using such entities from claiming treaty benefits, even though such investors would be subject to tax on the income derived through such entities. Paragraph 1 of the Memorandum of Understanding sets forth the understanding of the Contracting States that paragraph 6 applies to identify the person that derives an item of income, profit or gain paid to a fiscally transparent entity for purposes of applying the Convention to that first mention person. The provision also prevents a resident of a Contracting State from claiming treaty benefits in circumstances where the resident investing in the entity does not take into account the item of income paid to the entity because the entity is not fiscally transparent in its State of residence.

In general, the principles incorporated in this paragraph reflect the regulations under Treas. Reg. 1.894-1(d). Treas. Reg. 1.894-1(d)(3)(iii) provides that an entity will be fiscally transparent under the laws of an interest holder's jurisdiction with respect to an item of income to the extent that the laws of that jurisdiction require the interest holder resident in that jurisdiction to separately take into account on a current basis the interest holder's respective share of the item of income paid to the entity, whether or not distributed to the interest holder, and the character and source of the item in the hands of the interest holder are determined as if such item were realized directly by the interest holder. Entities falling under this description in the United States include partnerships, corporations that have made a valid election to be taxed under Subchapter S of Chapter 1 of the Code ("S corporations"), common investment trusts under section 584, simple trusts and grantor trusts. This paragraph also applies to payments made to other entities, such as U.S. limited liability companies ("LLCs"), that may be treated as either partnerships or as disregarded entities for U.S. tax purposes.

New paragraph 6 provides that, for purposes of applying the Convention, an item of income, profit or gain derived through an entity that is fiscally transparent under the laws of either Contracting State, and that is formed or organized in either Contracting State, or in a state that has an agreement in force containing a provision for the exchange of information on tax matters with the Contracting State from which the income, profit or gain is derived, shall be considered to be derived by a resident of a Contracting State to the extent that the item is treated for purposes of the taxation law of such Contracting State as the income, profit or gain of a resident. For example, if a company that is a resident of Spain pays interest to an entity that is formed or organized either in the United States or in a country with which Spain has an agreement in force containing a provision for the exchange of information on tax matters, and that entity is treated as fiscally transparent for U.S. tax purposes, the interest will be considered derived by a resident of the United States, but only to the extent that the taxation laws of the United States treat one or more U.S. residents (whose status as U.S. residents is determined, for this purpose, under U.S. tax law) as deriving the interest for U.S. tax purposes. Where the entity is a partnership, the persons who are, under U.S. tax laws, treated as partners of the entity would normally be the persons whom the U.S. tax laws would treat as deriving the interest income through the partnership. Also, it follows that persons whom the United States treats as partners but who are not U.S. residents for U.S. tax purposes may not claim a benefit under the Convention for the interest paid to the partnership, because such third-country partners are not residents of the United States for purposes of claiming this benefit. If, however, the country in which the third-country partners are treated as residents for tax purposes, as determined under the laws of that country, has an income tax convention with the other Contracting State, they may be entitled to claim a benefit under that convention (these results would also follow in the case of an entity that is disregarded as an entity separate from its owner under the laws of one jurisdiction but not the other, such as a single-owner entity that is viewed as a branch for U.S. tax purposes and as a corporation for tax purposes under the laws of the other Contracting State). In contrast, where the entity is organized under U.S. laws and is classified as a corporation for U.S. tax purposes, interest paid by a company that is a resident of Spain to the U.S. corporation will be considered derived by a resident of the United States since the U.S. corporation is treated under U.S. taxation laws as a resident of the United States and as deriving the income.

The same result would be reached even if the tax laws of Spain would treat the entity differently (e.g., if the entity were not treated as fiscally transparent in Spain in the first example above where the entity is treated as a partnership for U.S. tax purposes). Similarly, the characterization of the entity by a third country is also irrelevant, even if the entity is organized in that third country, although in such cases, subparagraph 6(b) requires that an agreement containing a provision for the exchange of information be in force between the source State and the third country.

These principles also apply to trusts to the extent that they are wholly or partly fiscally transparent in either Contracting State. For example, suppose that X, a resident of Spain, creates a revocable trust in the United States and names persons resident in a third country as the beneficiaries of the trust. If, under the laws of Spain, X is treated as taking the trust's income into account for tax purposes, the trust's income would be regarded as being derived by a resident of Spain. In contrast, since the determination of deriving an item of income, profit or gain is made on an item by item basis, it is possible that, in the case of a U.S. non-grantor trust, the trust itself may be able to claim benefits with respect to certain items of income, such as capital gains, so long as it is a resident liable to tax on such gains, but not with respect to other items of income that are treated as income of the trust's interest holders.

As noted above, paragraph 6 is not an exception to the saving clause of paragraph 4. Accordingly, paragraph 6 does not prevent a Contracting State from taxing an entity that is treated as a resident of that State under its tax law. For example, if a U.S. LLC with members who are residents of Spain elects to be taxed as a corporation for U.S. tax purposes, the United States will tax that LLC on its worldwide income on a net basis, without regard to whether Spain views the LLC as fiscally transparent.

Paragraph 1 of the Memorandum of Understanding sets forth the understanding of the Contracting States regarding the relationship of paragraph 6 with the other provisions of the Convention. In order to obtain the benefits of the Convention with respect to an item of income, the person who according to paragraph 6 derives an item of income must satisfy all applicable requirements specified in the Convention, including other applicable requirements of Article 1, the requirements of Article 4 (Residence), Article 17 (Limitation on Benefits) and the concepts of beneficial ownership found in Articles 10 (Dividends), 11 (Interest) and 12 (Royalties).

Article II

Article II of the Protocol amends Article 3 (General Definitions) of the existing Convention.

Paragraph 1

Paragraph 1 adds a new subparagraph (j) to paragraph 1 of Article 3. Subparagraph 1(j) defines the term "pension fund". Clause 1(j)(i) provides that in the case of Spain, the term means any scheme, fund, mutual benefit institution or other entity established in Spain that satisfies two criteria. First, as provided in clause 1(j)(i)(A), the person must be operated principally to manage the right of its beneficiaries to receive income or capital upon retirement, survivorship, widowhood, orphanhood, or disability. Second, contributions to the pension fund must be deductible from the taxable base of personal taxes.

Subparagraph 3(a) of the Memorandum of Understanding as corrected by the Exchange of Notes sets forth a non-exhaustive descriptive list of those U.S. entities that will be regarded as pension funds for purposes of the Convention. The list includes: a trust providing pension or retirement benefits under an Internal Revenue Code section 401(a) qualified pension plan (which includes a Code section 401(k) plan), a profit sharing or stock bonus plan, a Code section 403(a) qualified annuity plan, a Code section 403(b) plan, a trust that is an individual retirement account under Code section 408, a Roth individual retirement account under Code section 408A, a simple retirement account under Code section 408(p), a trust providing pension or retirement benefits under a simplified employee pension plan under Code section 408(k), a trust described in section 457(g) providing pension or retirement benefits under a Code section 457(b) plan, and the Thrift Savings Fund (section 7701(j)). A group trust described in Revenue Ruling 81-100, as amended by Revenue Ruling 2004-67 and Revenue Ruling 2011-1, shall qualify as a pension fund only if it earns income principally for the benefit of one or more pension funds that are themselves entitled to benefits under the Convention as residents of the United States.

Subparagraph 3(b) of the Memorandum of Understanding sets forth a non-exhaustive descriptive list of those Spanish entities that will be regarded as pension funds for purposes of the Convention. The list includes: 1) any fund regulated under the Amended Test of the Law on pension funds and pension schemes (*Texto Refundido de la Ley sobre Fondos y Planes de Pensiones*), passed by Legislative Royal Decree 1/2002 of November 29; 2) any entity defined under Article 64 of the Amended Text of the Law on the regulation and monitoring of private insurances (*Texto Refundido de la Ley de Ordenación y Supervisión de los Seguros Privados*) passed by Legislative Royal Decree 6/2004 of October 29, provided that in the case of mutual funds all participants are employees; promoters and sponsoring partners are the companies, institutions or individual entrepreneurs to which the employees are engaged; and benefits are exclusively derived from the social welfare agreement between both parties, as well as any other comparable entity regulated within the scope of the political subdivisions (*Comunidades Autónomas*); and 3) insurance companies regulated under the Amended Text of the Law on the regulation and monitoring of private insurances passed by

Legislative Royal Decree 6/2004 of October 29 whose activity is the coverage of the contingencies provided for in the Amended Text of the Law on pension funds and pension schemes.

Clause 1(j)(ii) of new subparagraph 1(j) of Article 3 provides that in the case of the United States, the term "pension fund" means any person established in the United States that is generally exempt from income taxation in the United States, and is operated principally either to administer or provide pension or retirement benefits, or to earn income principally for the benefit of one or more persons established in the same Contracting State that are generally exempt from income taxation in that Contracting State and are operated principally to administer or provide pension or retirement benefits.

The definition, as it applies in the case of the United States, recognizes that pension funds sometimes administer or provide benefits other than pension or retirement benefits, such as death benefits. However, in order for the fund to be considered a pension fund for purposes of the Convention, the provision of any other such benefits must be merely incidental to the fund's principal activity of administering or providing pension or retirement benefits. The definition also ensures that if a fund is a collective fund that earns income for the benefit of other funds, then substantially all of the funds that participate in the collective fund must be residents of the same Contracting State as the collective fund and must be entitled to benefits under the Convention in their own right.

Paragraph 2

Paragraph 2 replaces paragraph 2 of Article 3 of the existing Convention. Terms that are not defined in the existing Convention are dealt with in paragraph 2.

New paragraph 2 of Article 3 provides that in the application of the Convention, any term used but not defined in the Convention will have the meaning that it has under the domestic law of the Contracting State applying the Convention, unless the context requires otherwise, and subject to the provisions of Article 26 (Mutual Agreement Procedure). If the term is defined under both the tax and non-tax laws of a Contracting State, the definition in the tax law will take precedence over the definition in the non-tax laws. Finally, there also may be cases where the tax laws of a State contain multiple definitions of the same term. In such a case, the definition used for purposes of the particular provision at issue, if any, should be used.

The reference in paragraph 2 to the domestic law of a Contracting State means the law in effect at the time the treaty is being applied, not the law as in effect at the time the treaty was signed. The use of "ambulatory" definitions, however, may lead to results that are at variance with the intentions of the negotiators and of the Contracting States when the treaty was negotiated and ratified. The inclusion in both paragraphs 1 and 2 of an exception to the generally applicable definitions where the "context otherwise requires" is intended to address this circumstance. Where reflecting the intent of the Contracting States requires the use of a definition that is different from a definition under paragraph 1 or the law of the Contracting State applying the Convention, that definition will apply. Thus, flexibility in defining terms is necessary and permitted.

Article III

Article III of the Protocol replaces paragraph 3 of Article 5 (Permanent Establishment) of the existing Convention. Paragraph 3 of Article 5 provides rules to determine whether a building site or a construction, assembly or installation project, or an installation or drilling rig or ship used for the exploration of natural resources constitutes a permanent establishment for the contractor, driller, etc. Such a site or activity does not create a permanent establishment unless the site, project, etc. lasts, or the exploration activity continues, for more than twelve months. It is only necessary to refer to "exploration" and not "exploitation" in this context because exploitation activities are defined to constitute a permanent establishment under subparagraph (f) of paragraph 2 of Article 5. Thus, a drilling rig does not constitute a permanent establishment if a well is drilled in less than twelve months. However, the well becomes a permanent establishment as of the date that production begins.

The twelve-month test applies separately to each site or project. The twelve-month period begins when work (including preparatory work carried on by the enterprise) physically begins in a Contracting State. A series of contracts or projects by a contractor that are interdependent both commercially and geographically are to be treated as a single project for purposes of applying the twelve-month threshold test. For example, the construction of a housing development would be considered as a single project even if each house were constructed for a different purchaser.

In applying this paragraph, time spent by a sub-contractor on a building site is counted as time spent by the general contractor at the site for purposes of determining whether the general contractor has a permanent establishment. However, for the sub-contractor itself to be treated as having a permanent establishment, the sub-contractor's activities at the site must last for more than twelve months. For purposes of applying the twelve-month rule, time is measured from the first day the sub-contractor is on the site until the last day. Thus, if a sub-contractor is on a site intermittently, intervening days that the sub-contractor is not on the site are counted.

These interpretations of the Article are based on the Commentary to paragraph 3 of Article 5 of the OECD Model, which contains language that is substantially the same as that in the Convention. These interpretations are consistent with the generally accepted international interpretation of the relevant language in paragraph 3 of Article 5 of the Convention.

If the twelve-month threshold is exceeded, the site or project constitutes a permanent establishment from the first day of activity.

Article IV

Article IV of the Protocol replaces Article 10 (Dividends) of the existing Convention. New Article 10 provides rules for the taxation of dividends paid by a company that is a resident of one Contracting State to a beneficial owner that is a resident of the other Contracting State. The Article provides for full residence-State taxation of such dividends and limitations on (including, in some cases, a prohibition from) taxation by the source State. New Article 10 also provides rules for the imposition of a tax on branch profits by the State of source. Finally, the Article prohibits a State from imposing taxes on a company resident in the other Contracting State, other than a branch profits tax, on undistributed earnings.

Paragraph 1 of New Article 10

Paragraph 1 of new Article 10 permits a Contracting State to tax its residents on dividends paid to them by a company that is a resident of the other Contracting State. For dividends from any other source paid to a resident, Article 23 (Other Income) of the Convention grants the residence country exclusive taxing jurisdiction (other than for dividends attributable to a permanent establishment in the other State).

Paragraph 2 of New Article 10

The State of source also may tax dividends beneficially owned by a resident of the other State, subject to the limitations of paragraphs 2, 3 and 4. Paragraph 2 of new Article 10 generally limits the rate of withholding tax in the State of source on dividends paid by a company resident in that State to 15 percent of the gross amount of the dividend. If, however, the beneficial owner of the dividend is a company resident in the other State and owns directly shares representing at least 10 percent of the voting power of the company paying the dividend, then the rate of withholding tax in the State of source is limited to 5 percent of the gross amount of the dividend. For application of this paragraph by the United States, shares are considered voting stock if they provide the power to elect, appoint or replace any person vested with the powers ordinarily exercised by the board of directors of a U.S. corporation.

The determination of whether the ownership threshold for subparagraph 2(a) is met for purposes of the 5 percent maximum rate of withholding tax is made on the date on which entitlement to the dividend is determined. Thus, in the case of a dividend from a U.S. company, the determination of whether the ownership threshold is met generally would be made on the dividend record date.

Paragraph 2 does not affect the taxation of the profits out of which the dividends are paid. The taxation by a Contracting State of the income of its resident companies is governed by the domestic law of the Contracting State, subject to the provisions of paragraph 4 of Article 25 (Non-Discrimination).

The term "beneficial owner" is not defined in the Convention, and is, therefore, generally defined under the domestic law of the country imposing tax (*i.e.*, the source country). The beneficial owner of the dividend for purposes of Article 10 is the person to which the income is attributable under the laws of the source State. Thus, if a dividend paid by a corporation that is a resident of one of the States (as determined under Article 4 (Residence)) is received by a nominee or agent that is a resident of the other State on behalf of a person that is not a resident of that other State, the dividend is not entitled to the benefits of this Article. However, a dividend received by a nominee on behalf of a resident of that other State would be entitled to benefits. These limitations are supported by paragraphs 12-12.2 of the Commentary to Article 10 of the OECD Model.

Special rules apply to shares held through fiscally transparent entities both for purposes of determining whether the ownership threshold has been met and for purposes of determining the beneficial owner of the dividend.

A company that is a resident of a Contracting State shall be considered to own directly the voting stock owned by an entity that is considered fiscally transparent under the laws of that State and that is not a resident of the other Contracting State of which the company paying the dividends is a resident, in proportion to the company's ownership interest in that entity. This is consistent with the rules of paragraph 6 of Article 1 (General Scope) as revised by Article I, which provides that residence State principles shall be used to determine who derives the dividends, to ensure that the dividends for which the source State grants benefits of the Convention will be taken into account for tax purposes by a resident of the residence State.

For example, assume that FCo, a company that is a resident of the Spain, owns a 50 percent interest in FP, a partnership that is organized in Spain. FP owns 100 percent of the sole class of stock of USCo, a company resident in the United States. Spain views FP as fiscally transparent under its domestic law, and taxes FCo currently on its distributive share of the income of FP and determines the character and source of the income received through FP in the hands of FCo as if such income were realized directly by FCo. In this case, FCo is treated as deriving 50 percent of the dividends paid by USCo under paragraph 6 of Article 1. Moreover, FCo is treated as owning 50 percent of the stock of USCo directly. The same result would be reached even if the tax laws of the United States would treat FP differently (*e.g.*, if FP were not treated as fiscally transparent in the United States), or if FP were organized in a third state, provided that that state has an agreement in force containing a provision for the exchange of information on tax matters with Spain, which in this example is the Contracting State from which the dividend arises, and as long as FP were still treated as fiscally transparent under the laws of the United States.

While residence State principles control who is treated as owning voting stock of the company paying dividends through a fiscally transparent entity and, consequently, who derives the dividends, source State principles of beneficial ownership apply to determine whether the person who derives the dividends, or another resident of the other Contracting State, is the beneficial owner of the dividends. If the person who derives the dividends under paragraph 6 of Article 1 would not be treated as a nominee, agent, custodian, conduit, etc. under the source State's principles for determining beneficial ownership, that person will be treated as the beneficial owner of the dividends for purposes of the Convention. In the example above, FCo is required to satisfy the beneficial ownership principles of the United States with respect to the dividends it derives. If under the beneficial ownership principles of the United States, FCo is found not to be the beneficial owner of the dividends, FCo will not be entitled to the benefits of Article 10 with respect to such dividends. If FCo is found to be a nominee, agent, custodian, or conduit for a person who is a resident of the other Contracting State, that person may be entitled to benefits with respect to the dividends.

Paragraph 3 of New Article 10

Paragraph 3 of new Article 10 provides exclusive residence-country taxation (*i.e.,* an elimination of withholding tax) with respect to certain dividends distributed by a company that is a resident of one Contracting State to a resident of the other Contracting State. As described further below, this elimination of withholding tax is available with respect to certain inter-company dividends and with respect to certain pension funds.

Subparagraph 3(a) provides for the elimination of withholding tax on dividends beneficially owned by a company that has owned, directly or indirectly through one or more residents of either Contracting State, 80 percent or more of the voting power of the company paying the dividend for the twelve-month period ending on the date entitlement to the dividend is determined. The determination of whether the beneficial owner of the dividends owns at least 80 percent of the voting power of the company is made by taking into account stock owned both directly and indirectly through one or more residents of either Contracting State.

Eligibility for the elimination of withholding tax provided by subparagraph 3(a) is subject to additional restrictions based on, and supplementing, the rules of Article 17 (Limitation on Benefits) as that Article has been modified by Article IX. Accordingly, a company that meets the holding requirements described above will qualify for the benefits of paragraph 3 only if it also: (1) meets the "publicly traded" test of subparagraph 2(c) of Article 17, (2) meets the "ownership-base erosion" and "active trade or business" tests described in subparagraph 2(e) and paragraph 4 of Article 17, (3) meets the "derivative benefits" test of paragraph 3 of Article 17, or (4) is granted the benefits of paragraph 3 of Article 10 at the discretion of the competent authority of the source State pursuant to paragraph 7 of Article 17.

For example, assume that ThirdCo is a company resident in a third country that does not have a tax treaty with the United States providing for the elimination of withholding tax on inter-company dividends. ThirdCo owns directly 100 percent of the issued and outstanding voting stock of USCo, a U.S. company, and of SCo, a Spanish company. SCo is a substantial company that manufactures widgets. USCo distributes those widgets in the United States. If ThirdCo contributes to SCo all the stock of USCo, dividends paid by USCo to SCo would qualify for treaty benefits under the active trade or business test of paragraph 4 of Article 30. However, allowing ThirdCo to qualify for the elimination of withholding tax, which is not available to it under the third state's treaty with the United States (if any), would encourage treaty shopping.

In order to prevent this type of treaty shopping, paragraph 3 requires SCo to meet the ownership-base erosion requirements of subparagraph 2(e) of Article 17 as revised by Article IX in addition to the active trade or business test of paragraph 4 of Article 17. Because SCo is wholly owned by a third country resident, SCo could not qualify for the elimination of withholding tax on dividends from USCo under the combined ownership-base erosion and active trade or business tests of subparagraph 3(b). Consequently, SCo would need to qualify under another test in paragraph 3 or obtain discretionary relief from the competent authority under Article 17 paragraph 7. For purpose of subparagraph 3(b), it is not sufficient for a company to qualify for treaty benefits generally under the active trade or business test or the ownership-base erosion test unless it qualifies for treaty benefits under both.

Alternatively, companies that are publicly traded or subsidiaries of publicly-traded companies will generally qualify for the elimination of withholding tax. Thus, a company that is a resident of Spain and that meets the requirements of subparagraph 2(c) of Article 17 will be entitled to the elimination of withholding tax, subject to the ownership and holding period requirements.

In addition, under subparagraph 3(c), a company that is a resident of a Contracting State may also qualify for the elimination of withholding tax on dividends if it satisfies the derivative benefits test of paragraph 3 of Article 17, subject to the ownership and holding period requirements. Thus, a Spanish company that has owned all of the stock of a U.S. corporation for the twelve-month period ending on the date on which entitlement to the dividend is determined may qualify for the elimination of withholding tax if it is wholly-owned by a company that falls within the definition of "equivalent beneficiary" in subparagraph 8(g) of Article 17.

The derivative benefits test may also provide benefits to U.S. companies receiving dividends from Spanish subsidiaries because of the effect of the Parent-Subsidiary Directive in the European Union. Under that directive, inter-company dividends paid within the European Union are free of withholding tax. Under subparagraph 8(h) of Article 17 that directive will be taken into account in determining whether the owner of a U.S. company receiving dividends from a Spanish company is an equivalent beneficiary. Thus, a company that is a resident of a member state of the European Union will, by virtue of the Parent-Subsidiary Directive, satisfy the requirements of Article subparagraph 8(g)(i)(B) of Article 17 with respect to any dividends received by its U.S. subsidiary from a Spanish company. For example, assume USCo is a wholly-owned subsidiary of ICo, an Italian publicly-traded company. USCo owns all of the shares of SCo, a Spanish company. If SCo were to pay dividends directly to ICo, those dividends would be exempt from withholding tax in Spain by reason of the Parent-Subsidiary Directive. If ICo meets the other conditions to be an equivalent beneficiary under subparagraph 8(g) of Article 17, it will be treated as an equivalent beneficiary.

A company also may qualify for the elimination of withholding tax pursuant to subparagraph 3(c) if it is owned by seven or fewer U.S. or Spanish residents who qualify as an "equivalent beneficiary" and meet the other requirements of the derivative benefits provision. This rule may apply, for example, to certain Spanish corporate joint venture vehicles that are closely-held by a few Spanish resident individuals.

Subparagraph 8(g) of Article 17 contains a specific rule of application intended to ensure that for purposes of applying paragraph 3, certain joint ventures, not just wholly-owned subsidiaries, can qualify for benefits. For example, assume that the United States were to enter into a treaty with Country X, a member of the European Union, that includes a provision identical to paragraph 3. USCo is 100 percent owned by SCo, a Spanish company, which in turn is owned 49 percent by PCo, a Spanish publicly-traded company, and 51 percent by XCo, a publicly-traded company that is resident in Country X. In the absence of a special rule for interpreting the derivative benefits provision, each of PCo and XCo would be treated as owning only their proportionate share of the shares held by SCo in USCo. If that rule were applied in this situation, neither PCo nor XCo would be an equivalent beneficiary, because neither would meet the 80 percent ownership test with respect to USCo. However, since both PCo and XCo are residents of countries that have treaties with the United States that provide for elimination of withholding tax on inter-company dividends, it is appropriate to provide benefits to SCo in this case.

Accordingly, the definition of "equivalent beneficiary" includes a rule of application that is intended to ensure that such joint ventures qualify for the benefits of paragraph 3. Under that rule, each of the shareholders is treated as owning shares of USCo with the same percentage of voting power as the shares held by SCo for purposes of determining whether it would be entitled to an equivalent rate of withholding tax. This rule is necessary because of the high ownership threshold for qualification for the elimination of withholding tax on inter-company dividends.

If a company does not qualify for the elimination of withholding tax under any of the foregoing objective tests, it may request a determination from the relevant competent authority pursuant to paragraph 7 of Article 17.

Paragraph 4 of New Article 10

Paragraph 4 of new Article 10 provides that dividends beneficially owned by a pension fund may not be taxed in the Contracting State of which the company paying the tax is a resident, unless such dividends are derived from the carrying on of a business, directly or indirectly, by the pension fund or through an associated enterprise. For purposes of application of this paragraph by the United States, the term "trade or business" shall be defined in accordance with Code section 513(c). The term "pension fund" is defined in subparagraph 1(j) of Article 3 (General Definitions) of the Convention, as amended by Article II of the Protocol.

Paragraph 5 of New Article 10

Paragraph 5 of new Article 10 defines the term dividends broadly and flexibly. The definition is intended to cover all arrangements that yield a return on an equity investment in a corporation as determined under the tax law of the state of source, as well as arrangements that might be developed in the future.

The term includes income from shares, "jouissance" shares or "jouissance" rights, mining shares, founders' shares or other rights that are not treated as debt under the law of the source State, that participate in the profits of the company. The term also includes income that is subjected to the same tax treatment as income from shares by the law of the State of source, including amounts treated as dividend equivalents under Code section 871(m). Thus, a constructive dividend that results from a non-arm's length transaction between a corporation and a related party is a dividend. In the case of the United States the term dividend includes amounts treated as a dividend under U.S. law upon the sale or redemption of shares or upon a transfer of shares in a reorganization. *See* Rev. Rul. 92-85, 1992-2 C.B. 69 (sale of foreign subsidiary's stock to U.S. sister company is a deemed dividend to extent of the subsidiary's and sister company's earnings and profits). Further, a distribution from a U.S. publicly traded limited partnership, which is taxed as a corporation under U.S. law, is a dividend for purposes of Article 10. However, a distribution by a limited liability company is not taxable by the United States under Article 10, provided the limited liability company is not characterized as an association taxable as a corporation under U.S. law. Paragraph 5 also clarifies that the term "dividends" does not include distributions that are treated as gain under the laws of the State of which the company making the distribution is a resident. In such case, the provisions of Article 13 (Gains) shall apply (for example, the United States shall apply Code Section 897(h) and the regulations thereunder).

Finally, a payment denominated as interest that is made by a thinly capitalized corporation may be treated as a dividend to the extent that the debt is recharacterized as equity under the laws of the source State.

Paragraph 6 of New Article 10

Paragraph 6 of new Article 10 provides a rule for taxing dividends paid with respect to holdings that form part of the business property of a permanent establishment or fixed base. In such case, the rules of Article 7 (Business Profits) shall apply. Accordingly, the dividends will be taxed on a net basis using the rates and rules of taxation generally applicable to residents of the State in which the permanent establishment or fixed base is located, as such rules may be modified by the Convention. An example of dividends paid with respect to the business property of a permanent establishment would be dividends derived by a dealer in stock or securities from stock or securities that the dealer held for sale to customers.

Paragraph 7 of New Article 10

The right of a Contracting State to tax dividends paid by a company that is a resident of the other Contracting State is restricted by paragraph 7 of new Article 10 to cases in which the dividends are paid to a resident of that Contracting State or are effectively connected to a permanent establishment in that Contracting State. Thus, a

Contracting State may not impose a "secondary" withholding tax on dividends paid by a nonresident company out of earnings and profits from that Contracting State.

The paragraph also restricts the right of a Contracting State to impose corporate level taxes on undistributed profits, other than a branch profits tax. The paragraph does not restrict a State's right to tax its resident shareholders on undistributed earnings of a corporation resident in the other State. Thus, the authority of the United States to impose taxes on subpart F income and on earnings deemed invested in U.S. property, and its tax on income of a passive foreign investment company that is a qualified electing fund is in no way restricted by this provision.

Paragraph 8 of New Article 10

Paragraph 8 of new Article 10 permits a Contracting State to impose a branch profits tax on a company resident in the other Contracting State. The tax is in addition to other taxes permitted by the Convention. The term "company" is defined in subparagraph 1(e) of Article 3 (General Definitions) of the Convention.

A Contracting State may impose a branch profits tax on a company if the company has income attributable to a permanent establishment in that Contracting State, derives income from real property (immovable property) in that Contracting State that is taxed on a net basis under Article 6 (Income from Real Property (Immovable Property)), or realizes gains taxable in that State under paragraph 1 of Article 13 (Capital Gains). In the case of the United States, the imposition of such tax is limited, however, to the portion of the aforementioned items of income that represents the amount of such income that is the "dividend equivalent amount." The dividend equivalent amount for any year approximates the dividend that a U.S. branch office would have paid during the year if the branch had been operated as a separate U.S. subsidiary company. This is consistent with the relevant rules under the U.S. branch profits tax, and the term dividend equivalent amount is defined under U.S. law. Section 884 defines the dividend equivalent amount as an amount for a particular year that is equivalent to the income described above that is included in the corporation's effectively connected earnings and profits for that year, after payment of the corporate tax under Articles 6, 7 (Business Profits) or 13, reduced for any increase in the branch's U.S. net equity during the year or increased for any reduction in its U.S. net equity during the year. U.S. net equity is U.S. assets less U.S. liabilities. See Treas. Reg. 1.884-1. The amount analogous to the dividend equivalent amount in the case of Spain is the amount of income (*Imposición Complementaria*) determined under the Spanish Non Residents Income Tax regulated by the Amended Text of Non Residents Income Tax Law, passed by Legislative Royal Decree 5/2004 of 5th March, as it may be amended from time to time.

As discussed in the Technical Explanation to paragraph 2 of Article 1 (General Scope), consistency principles prohibit a taxpayer from applying provisions of the Code and this Convention in an inconsistent manner in order to minimize tax. In the context of the branch profits tax, this consistency requirement means that if a company resident in Spain uses the principles of Article 7 to determine its U.S. taxable income, it must then also use those principles to determine its dividend equivalent amount. Similarly, if the company instead uses the Code to determine its U.S. taxable income it must also use the Code to determine its dividend equivalent amount. As in the case of Article 7, if a Spanish company, for example, does not from year to year consistently apply the Code or the Convention to determine its dividend equivalent amount, then the company must make appropriate adjustments or recapture amounts that would otherwise be subject to U.S. branch profits tax if it had consistently applied the Code or the Convention to determine its dividend equivalent amount from year to year.

Paragraph 9 of New Article 10

Paragraph 9 of new Article 10 limits the rate of the branch profits tax that may be imposed under paragraph 8 to 5 percent, as provided in subparagraph 2(a) of Article 10. Paragraph 9 also provides that the branch profits tax shall not be imposed on a company in any case if certain requirements are met. In general, these requirements provide rules for a branch that parallel the rules for when a dividend paid by a subsidiary will be subject to exclusive residence-country taxation (*i.e.*, the elimination of source-country withholding tax). Accordingly, the branch profits tax cannot be imposed in the case of a company that satisfies any of the following requirements set forth in Article 17 (Limitation on Benefits) as revised by Article IX: (1) the "publicly traded" test of subparagraph 2(c); (2) both the "ownership-base erosion" and "active trade or business" tests described in subparagraph 2(e) and paragraph 4; (3) the "derivative benefits" test of paragraph 3; or (4) paragraph 7. If the company did not meet any of those tests, but otherwise qualified for benefits under Article 17, then the branch profits tax would apply at a rate of 5 percent as provided in subparagraph 2(a).

Paragraph 9 applies equally if a taxpayer determines its taxable income under the laws of a Contracting State or under the provisions of Article 7 (Business Profits). For example, as discussed above, consistency principles require a company resident in Spain that determines its U.S. taxable income under the Code to also determine its dividend equivalent amount under the Code. In that case, the withholding rate reduction provided in subparagraph 2(a) would apply even though the company did not determine its dividend equivalent amount using the principles of Article 7.

Article V

Article V of the Protocol replaces Article 11 (Interest) of the existing Convention. New Article 11 specifies the taxing jurisdictions over interest income of the States of source and residence and defines the terms necessary to apply the Article.

Paragraph 1 of New Article 11

Paragraph 1 of new Article 11 generally grants to the State of residence the exclusive right to tax interest beneficially owned by its residents and arising in the other Contracting State.

The term "beneficial owner" is not defined in the Convention, and is, therefore, defined under the domestic law of the State of source. The beneficial owner of the interest for purposes of Article 11 is the person to which the income is attributable under the laws of the source State. Thus, if interest arising in a Contracting State is received by a nominee or agent that is a resident of the other State on behalf of a person that is not a resident of that other State, the interest is not entitled to the benefits of Article 11. However, interest received by a nominee on behalf of a resident of that other State would be entitled to benefits. These limitations are confirmed by paragraph 9 of the OECD Commentary to Article 11.

Special rules apply to interest derived through fiscally transparent entities for purposes of determining the beneficial owner of the interest. In such cases, residence State principles shall be used to determine who derives the interest, to assure that the interest for which the source State grants benefits of the Convention will be taken into account for tax purposes by a resident of the residence State.

For example, assume that FCo, a company that is a resident of Spain, owns a 50 percent interest in FP, a partnership that is organized in Spain. FP receives interest arising in the United States. Spain views FP as fiscally transparent under its domestic law, and taxes FCo currently on its distributive share of the income of FP and determines the character and source of the income received through FP in the hands of FCo as if such income were realized directly by FCo. In this case, FCo is treated as deriving 50 percent of the interest received by FP that arises in the United States under paragraph 6 of Article 1. The same result would be reached even if the tax laws of the United States would treat FP differently (*e.g.*, if FP were not treated as fiscally transparent in the United States), or if FP were organized in a third state, provided such state has an agreement in force containing a provision for the exchange of information on tax matters with Spain, which in this example is the Contracting State from which the interest arises, and as long as FP were still treated as fiscally transparent under the laws of the United States.

While residence State principles control who is treated as deriving the interest, source State principles of beneficial ownership apply to determine whether the person who derives the interest, or another resident of the other Contracting State, is the beneficial owner of the interest. If the person who derives the interest under paragraph 6 of Article 1 would not be treated as a nominee, agent, custodian, conduit, etc. under the source State's principles for determining beneficial ownership, that person will be treated as the beneficial owner of the interest for purposes of the Convention. In the example above, FCo is required to satisfy the beneficial ownership principles of the United States with respect to the interest it derives. If under the beneficial ownership principles of the United States, FCo is found not to be the beneficial owner of the interest, FCo will not be entitled to the benefits of Article 11 with respect to such interest. If FCo is found to be a nominee, agent, custodian, or conduit for a person who is a resident of the other Contracting State, that person may be entitled to benefits with respect to the interest.

Paragraph 2 of New Article 11

Paragraph 2 of new Article 11 provides anti-abuse exceptions to the source-country exemption in paragraph 1 for two classes of interest payments arising in the United States.

The first class of interest, dealt with in subparagraph 2(a) is so-called "contingent interest" that does not qualify as portfolio interest under U.S. domestic law as defined in Code section 871(h)(4). The exceptions of section 871(h)(4)(c) will be applicable. If the beneficial owner of the contingent interest is a resident of Spain, subparagraph 2(a) provides that the gross amount of the interest may be taxed at a rate not exceeding 10 percent.

The second class of interest is dealt with in subparagraph 2(b). This exception is consistent with the policy of Code sections 860E(e) and 860G(b) that excess inclusions with respect to a real estate mortgage investment conduit (REMIC) should bear full U.S. tax in all cases. Without a full tax at source foreign purchasers of residual interests would have a competitive advantage over U.S. purchasers at the time these interests are initially offered. Also, absent this rule, the U.S. fisc would suffer a revenue loss with respect to mortgages held in a REMIC because of opportunities for tax avoidance created by differences in the timing of taxable and economic income produced by these interests.

Paragraph 3 of New Article 11

Paragraph 3 of new Article 11 provides a definition of the term "interest" for purposes of the Article that is essentially identical to that provided in paragraph 4 of Article 11 of the existing Convention. The term "interest" as used in Article 11 is defined in paragraph 3 to include, *inter alia*, income from debt claims of every kind, whether or not secured by a mortgage and whether or not carrying a right to participate in the debtor's profits. The term does not, however, include amounts that are treated as dividends under Article 10 (Dividends), nor does it include penalty charges for late payment.

The term interest also includes amounts subject to the same tax treatment as income from money lent under the law of the State in which the income arises. Thus, for purposes of the Convention, amounts that the United States will treat as interest include (i) the difference between the issue price and the stated redemption price at maturity of a debt instrument (*i.e.*, original issue discount ("OID")), which may be wholly or partially realized on the disposition of a debt instrument (section 1273), (ii) amounts that are imputed interest on a deferred sales contract (section 483), (iii) amounts treated as interest or OID under the stripped bond rules (section 1286), (iv) amounts treated as original issue discount under the below-market interest rate rules (section 7872), (v) a partner's distributive share of a partnership's interest income (section 702), (vi) the interest portion of periodic payments made under a "finance lease" or similar contractual arrangement that in substance is a borrowing by the nominal lessee to finance the acquisition of property, (vii) amounts included in the income of a holder of a residual interest in a REMIC (section 860E), because these amounts generally are subject to the same taxation treatment as interest under U.S. tax law, and (viii) interest with respect to notional principal contracts that are recharacterized as loans because of a "substantial non-periodic payment."

Paragraph 4 of New Article 11

Paragraph 4 of new Article 11 is identical in substance to paragraph 5 of Article 11 of the existing Convention. Paragraph 4 provides an exception to the exclusive residence taxation rule of paragraph 1 and the source State gross taxation rule of paragraph 2 in cases where the beneficial owner of the interest carries on or has carried on business through a permanent establishment situated in that State, or performs or has performed independent personal services through a fixed base situated in that state, and the debt-claim in respect of which the interest is paid is effectively connected with such permanent establishment or fixed base. In such cases the provisions of Article 7 (Business Profits) or Article 15 (Independent Personal Servicers), as the case may be, will apply and the State of source will retain the right to impose tax on such interest income.

In the case of a permanent establishment or fixed base that once existed in a Contracting State but no longer exists, the provisions of this paragraph shall apply to interest paid with respect to a debt-claim that would be effectively connected to such a permanent establishment or fixed base if it did exist in the year of payment or accrual. Accordingly, such interest would remain taxable under the provisions of Article 7 or 15, as the case may be, and not under this Article.

Paragraph 5 of New Article 11

Paragraph 5 of new Article 11 provides a source rule for interest that is identical in substance to the interest source rule of the existing Convention. Interest is considered to arise in a Contracting State if paid by a resident of that State. However, interest that is borne by a permanent establishment or fixed base in one of the Contracting States is considered to arise in that State. For this purpose, interest is considered to be borne by a permanent establishment or fixed base if it is allocable to taxable income of that permanent establishment or fixed base. If the actual amount of interest on the books of a U.S. branch of a resident of Spain exceeds the amount of interest allocated to the branch under Treas. Reg. 1.882-5, the amount of such excess will not be considered U.S. source interest for purposes of this Article.

Paragraph 6 of New Article 11

Paragraph 6 of new Article 11 is identical to paragraph 7 of Article 11 of the existing Convention. Paragraph 5 provides that in cases involving special relationships between the payor and the beneficial owner of interest income, Article 11 applies only to that portion of the total interest payments that would have been made absent such special relationships (*i.e.*, an arm's-length interest payment). Any excess amount of interest paid remains taxable according to the laws of the United States and the other Contracting State, respectively, with due regard to the other provisions of the Convention. Thus, if the excess amount would be treated under the source country's law as a distribution of profits by a corporation, such amount could be taxed as a dividend rather than as interest, but the tax would be subject, if appropriate, to the rate limitations of paragraph 2 of Article 10 (Dividends).

The term "special relationship" is not defined in the Convention. In applying this paragraph the United States considers the term to include the relationships described in Article 9, which in turn corresponds to the definition of "control" for purposes of Code section 482.

This paragraph does not address cases where, owing to a special relationship between the payer and the beneficial owner or between both of them and some other person, the amount of the interest is less than an arm's-length amount. In those cases a transaction may be characterized to reflect its substance and interest may be imputed consistent with the definition of "interest" in paragraph 3. The United States would apply Code section 482 or 7872 to determine the amount of imputed interest in those cases.

Relation to Other Articles

Notwithstanding the foregoing limitations on source country taxation of interest, the saving clause of subparagraph 3 of Article 1 (General Scope) permits the United States to tax its residents and citizens, subject to the special foreign tax credit rules of paragraph 3 of Article 24 (Relief from Double Taxation), as if the Convention had not come into force.

The benefits of this Article are also subject to the provisions of Article 17 (Limitation on Benefits). Thus, if a resident of Spain is the beneficial owner of interest paid by a U.S. corporation, the resident must qualify for treaty benefits under at least one of the tests of Article 17 in order to receive the benefits of this Article.

Article VI

Article VI of the Protocol replaces Article 12 (Royalties) of the existing Convention. New Article 12 provides rules for the taxation of royalties arising in one Contracting State and paid to a beneficial owner that is a resident of the other Contracting State.

Paragraph 1 of New Article 12

Paragraph 1 of new Article 12 generally grants to the State of residence the exclusive right to tax royalties beneficially owned by its residents and arising in the other Contracting State.

The term "beneficial owner" is not defined in the Convention, and is, therefore, defined under the domestic law of the State of source. The beneficial owner of the royalties for purposes of Article 12 is the person to which the income is attributable under the laws of the source State. Thus, if royalties arising in a Contracting State are received by a nominee or agent that is a resident of the other State on behalf of a person that is not a resident of that other State, the royalties are not entitled to the benefits of Article 12. However, the royalties received by a nominee on behalf of a resident of that other State would be entitled to benefits. These limitations are confirmed by paragraph 4 of the OECD Commentary to Article 12.

Special rules apply to royalties derived through fiscally transparent entities for purposes of determining the beneficial owner of the royalties. In such cases, residence State principles shall be used to determine who derives the royalties, to assure that the royalties for which the source State grants benefits of the Convention will be taken into account for tax purposes by a resident of the residence State.

For example, assume that FCo, a company that is a resident of Spain, owns a 50 percent interest in FP, a partnership that is organized in Spain. FP receives royalties arising in the United States. Spain views FP as fiscally transparent under its domestic law, and taxes FCo currently on its distributive share of the income of FP and determines the character and source of the income received through FP in the hands of FCo as if such income were realized directly by FCo. In this case, FCo is treated as deriving 50 percent of the royalties received by FP that arise in the United States under paragraph 6 of Article 1. The same result would be reached even if the tax laws of the United States would treat FP differently (*e.g.*, if FP were not treated as fiscally transparent in the United States), or if FP were organized in a third state, provided that that state has an agreement in force containing a provision for the exchange of information on tax matters with Spain, which in this example is the the Contracting State from which the royalty arises, and as long as FP were still treated as fiscally transparent under the laws of the United States.

While residence State principles control who is treated as deriving the royalties, source State principles of beneficial ownership apply to determine whether the person who derives the royalties, or another resident of Spain, is the beneficial owner of the royalties. If the person who derives the royalties under paragraph 6 of Article 1 would not be treated as a nominee, agent, custodian, conduit, etc. under the source State's principles for determining beneficial ownership, that person will be treated as the beneficial owner of the royalties for purposes of the Convention. In the example above, FCo is required to satisfy the beneficial ownership principles of the United States with respect to the royalties it derives. If under the beneficial ownership principles of the United States, FCo is found not to be the beneficial owner of the royalties, FCo will not be entitled to the benefits of Article 12 with respect to such royalties. If FCo is found to be a nominee, agent, custodian, or conduit for a person who is a resident of Spain, that person may be entitled to benefits with respect to the royalties.

Paragraph 2 of New Article 12

Paragraph 2 of new Article 12 defines the term "royalties," as used in Article 12, to include any consideration for the use of, or the right to use, any copyright of literary, artistic scientific or other work (including cinematographic films, and films and recordings for radio or television broadcasting), any patent, trademark, design or model, plan, secret formula or process, or for information concerning industrial, commercial, or scientific experience. The term "royalties" does not include income from leasing personal property.

The term royalties is defined in the Convention and therefore is generally independent of domestic law. Certain terms used in the definition are not defined in the Convention, but these may be defined under domestic tax law. For example, the term "secret process or formula" is found in the Code, and its meaning has been elaborated in the context of sections 351 and 367. *See* Rev. Rul. 55-17, 1955-1 C.B. 388; Rev. Rul. 64-56, 1964-1 C.B. 133; Rev. Proc. 69- 19, 1969-2 C.B. 301.

Consideration for the use or right to use cinematographic films, or works on film, tape, or other means of reproduction in radio or television broadcasting is specifically included in the definition of royalties. It is intended that, with respect to any subsequent technological advances in the field of radio or television broadcasting, consideration received for the use of such technology will also be included in the definition of royalties.

If an artist who is resident in one Contracting State records a performance in the other Contracting State, retains a copyrighted interest in a recording, and receives payments for the right to use the recording based on the sale or public playing of the recording, then the right of such other Contracting State to tax those payments is governed by Article 12. *See* Boulez v. Commissioner, 83 T.C. 584 (1984), aff'd, 810 F.2d 209 (D.C. Cir. 1986). By contrast, if the artist earns in the other Contracting State income covered by Article 19 (Artistes and Athletes), for example, endorsement income from the artist's attendance at a film screening, and if such income also is attributable to one of the rights described in Article 12 (*e.g.*, the use of the artist's photograph in promoting the screening), Article 19 and not Article 12 is applicable to such income.

Computer software generally is protected by copyright laws around the world. Under the Convention, consideration received for the use, or the right to use, computer software is treated either as royalties or as business profits, depending on the facts and circumstances of the transaction giving rise to the payment.

The primary factor in determining whether consideration received for the use, or the right to use, computer software is treated as royalties or as business profits is the nature of the rights transferred. *See* Treas. Reg. 1.861-18. The fact that the transaction is characterized as a license for copyright law purposes is not dispositive. For example, a typical retail sale of "shrink wrap" software generally will not be considered to give rise to royalty income, even though for copyright law purposes it may be characterized as a license.

The means by which the computer software is transferred are not relevant for purposes of the analysis. Consequently, if software is electronically transferred but the rights obtained by the transferee are substantially equivalent to rights in a program copy, the payment will be considered business profits.

The term "industrial, commercial, or scientific experience" (sometimes referred to as "know-how") has the meaning ascribed to it in paragraph 11 *et seq.* of the Commentary to Article 12 of the OECD Model. Consistent with that meaning, the term may include information that is ancillary to a right otherwise giving rise to royalties, such as a patent or secret process.

Know-how also may include, in limited cases, technical information that is conveyed through technical or consultancy services. It does not include general educational training of the user's employees, nor does it include information developed especially for the user, such as a technical plan or design developed according to the user's specifications. Thus, as provided in paragraph 11.3 of the Commentary to Article 12 of the OECD Model, the term "royalties" does not include payments received as consideration for after-sales service, for services rendered by a seller to a purchaser under a warranty, or for pure technical assistance.

The term "royalties" also does not include payments for professional services (such as architectural, engineering, legal, managerial, medical or software development services). For example, income from the design of a refinery by an engineer (even if the engineer employed know-how in the process of rendering the design) or the production of a legal brief by a lawyer is not income from the transfer of know-how taxable under Article 12, but is income from services taxable under either Article 15 (Independent Personal Services) or Article 16 (Dependent Personal Services) as applicable. Professional services may be embodied in property that gives rise to royalties, however. Thus, if a professional contracts to develop patentable property and retains rights in the resulting property under the development contract, subsequent license payments made for those rights would be royalties.

Paragraph 3 of New Article 12

This paragraph provides an exception to the rule of paragraph 1 that gives the State of residence exclusive taxing jurisdiction in cases where the beneficial owner of the royalties carries on or has carried on a business through a permanent establishment or performs or has performed personal services from a fixed base in the state of source and the right or property in respect of which the royalties are paid is effectively connected with that permanent establishment or fixed base. In such cases the provisions of Article 7 (Business Profits) or Article 15 (Independent Personal Services) will apply.

In the case of a permanent establishment that once existed in a Contracting State but that no longer exists, the provisions of this paragraph also apply to royalties paid with respect to rights or property that would be effectively connected to such permanent establishment if it did exist in the year of payment or accrual. Accordingly, such royalties would remain taxable under the provisions of Article 7, and not under this Article.

Paragraph 4 of New Article 12

Paragraph 4 of new Article 12 provides that in cases involving special relationships between the payor and beneficial owner of royalties, Article 12 applies only to the extent the royalties would have been paid absent such special relationships (*i.e.*, an arm's-length royalty). Any excess amount of royalties paid remains taxable according to the laws of the two Contracting States, with due regard to the other provisions of the Convention. If, for example, the excess amount is treated as a distribution of corporate profits under domestic law, such excess amount will be taxed as a dividend rather than as royalties, but the tax imposed on the dividend payment will be subject to the rate limitations of paragraph 2 of Article 10 (Dividends).

Relationship to Other Articles

Notwithstanding the foregoing limitations on source country taxation of royalties, the saving clause of paragraph 3 of Article 1 (General Scope) permits the United States to tax its residents and citizens, subject to the special foreign tax credit rules of paragraph 3 of Article 24 (Relief from Double Taxation), as if the Convention had not come into force.

As with other benefits of the Convention, the benefits of exclusive residence State taxation of royalties under paragraph 1 of Article 12 are available to a resident of the other State only if that resident is entitled to those benefits under Article 17 (Limitation on Benefits).

Article VII

Article VII of the Protocol makes amendments to Article 13 (Capital Gains) of the existing Convention.

Paragraph 1

Paragraph 1 of Article VII replaces paragraph 4 of existing Article 13. Because of the deletion of paragraph 4 of the existing Article, gains from the alienation of stock, participations or other rights in the capital of a company shall be taxed in accordance with the general rules of the Article. Revised paragraph 4 reflects Spain's prevailing tax treaty policy. Under the paragraph, a Contracting State may tax the gain from the alienation of shares of other rights, which directly or indirectly entitled the owner of such shares or rights to the enjoyment of immovable property situated in such Contracting State.

Paragraph 2

Paragraph 2 replaces paragraphs 6 and 7 of Article 13 of the existing Convention. New paragraph 6 of revised Article 13 provides that gains from the alienation of any property other than property referred to in paragraph 1 through 5 will be taxable only in the state of residence of the person alienating the property.

Article VIII

In a conforming change to the restatement of Article 10 (Dividends) of the existing Convention under Article IV of the Protocol, Article VIII of the Protocol deletes Article 14 (Branch Tax) of the existing Convention.

Article IX

Article IX of the Protocol replaces Article 17 (Limitation on Benefits) of the existing Convention. New Article 17 contains anti-treaty-shopping provisions that are intended to prevent residents of third countries from benefiting from what is intended to be a reciprocal agreement between two countries. In general, the provision does not rely on a determination of purpose or intention but instead sets forth a series of objective tests. A resident of a Contracting State that satisfies one of the tests will receive benefits regardless of its motivations in choosing its particular business structure.

The structure of the revised Article is as follows: Paragraph 1 states the general rule that residents are entitled to benefits otherwise accorded to residents only to the extent provided in the Article. Paragraph 2 lists a series of attributes of a resident of a Contracting State, the presence of any one of which will entitle that person to all the benefits of the Convention. Paragraph 3 provides a derivative benefits rule. Paragraph 4 provides that, regardless of whether a person qualifies for benefits under paragraph 2, benefits may be granted to that person with regard to certain income earned in the conduct of an active trade or business. Paragraph 5 provides a test for headquarters companies. Paragraph 6 provides a special rule for so-called "triangular cases" notwithstanding the other provisions of new Article 17. Paragraph 7 sets forth rules for the competent authorities of the Contracting States to apply to determine if a resident which cannot satisfy any of the tests in paragraphs 2, 3, 4 or 5 should nevertheless be entitled to a benefits provided in the Convention. Paragraph 8 defines certain terms used in the Article.

Paragraph 1 of New Article 17

Paragraph 1 of new Article 17 provides that a resident of a Contracting State will be entitled to the benefits otherwise accorded to residents of a Contracting State under the Convention only to the extent provided in the Article. The benefits otherwise accorded to residents under the Convention include all limitations on source-based taxation under Articles 6 (Income from Real Property (Immovable Property) through 16 (Dependent Personal Services) and 18 (Director's Fees) through 23 (Other Income), the treaty-based relief from double taxation provided by Article 24 (Relief from Double Taxation), and the protection afforded to residents of a Contracting State under Article 25 (Non-Discrimination). Some provisions do not require that a person be a resident in order to enjoy the benefits of those provisions. For example, Article 26 (Mutual Agreement Procedure) is not limited to residents of the Contracting States, and Article 28 (Diplomatic Agents and Consular Officers) applies to diplomatic agents or consular officials regardless of residence. Article 17 accordingly does not limit the availability of treaty benefits under these provisions.

Article 17 and the anti-abuse provisions of domestic law complement each other, as Article 17 effectively determines whether an entity has a sufficient nexus to the Contracting State to be treated as a resident for treaty purposes, while domestic anti-abuse provisions (*e.g.*, business purpose, substance-over-form, step transaction or conduit principles) determine whether a particular transaction should be recast in accordance with its substance. Thus, domestic law principles of the source Contracting State may be applied to identify the beneficial owner of an item of income, and Article 17 then will be applied to the beneficial owner to determine if that person is entitled to the benefits of the Convention with respect to such income.

Paragraph 2 of New Article 17

Paragraph 2 of new Article 17 has five subparagraphs, each of which describes a category of residents that will be considered qualified persons.

It is intended that the provisions of paragraph 2 will be self-executing. Unlike the provisions of paragraph 7 of the new Article, discussed below, claiming benefits under paragraph 2 does not require advance competent authority ruling or approval. The tax authorities may, of course, on review, determine that the taxpayer has improperly interpreted the paragraph and is not entitled to the benefits claimed.

Individuals -- Subparagraph 2(a)

Subparagraph 2(a) provides that individual residents of a Contracting State will be considered qualified persons. If such an individual receives income as a nominee on behalf of a third country resident, benefits may be denied under the applicable Articles of the Convention by the requirement that the beneficial owner of the income be a resident of a Contracting State.

Governments -- Subparagraph 2(b)

Subparagraph 2(b) provides that the Contracting States and any political subdivision or local authority or wholly-owned instrumentality thereof will be considered qualified persons.

Publicly-Traded Corporations -- Subparagraph 2(c)(i)

Subparagraph 2(c) applies to two categories of companies: publicly traded companies and subsidiaries of publicly traded companies. A company resident in a Contracting State will be considered a qualified person under clause (i) of subparagraph (c) if the principal class of its shares, and any disproportionate class of shares, is regularly traded on one or more recognized stock exchanges and the company satisfies at least one of the following additional requirements. First, under clause A) in the case of a company resident in Spain, the company's principal class of shares must be primarily traded on one or more recognized stock exchanges located either in Spain or within the European Union, and in the case of a company resident in the United States, the company's principal class or shares must be primarily traded on a recognized stock exchange located either in the United States or in another state that is a party to the North American Free Trade Agreement. If the company's principal class of shares does not satisfy the trading requirement set forth in clause A), clause B) provides that the regularly-traded company can nevertheless satisfy the requirements of clause (i) if the company's primary place of management and control is in its State of residence.

The term "recognized stock exchange" is defined in subparagraph 8(a) of revised Article 17. It includes (i) any stock exchange registered with the Securities and Exchange Commission as a national securities exchange for purposes of the Securities Exchange Act of 1934; (ii) any Spanish stock exchange controlled by the *Comisión Nacional del Mercado de Valores*; (iii) the principal stock exchanges of Stuttgart, Hamburg, Dusseldorf, Frankfurt, Berlin, Hannover, Munich, London, Amsterdam, Milan, Budapest, Lisbon, Toronto, Mexico City and Buenos Aires, and (iv) any other stock exchange agreed upon by the competent authorities of the Contracting States.

If a company has only one class of shares, it is only necessary to consider whether the shares of that class meet the relevant trading requirements. If the company has more than one class of shares, it is necessary as an initial matter to determine which class or classes constitute the "principal class of shares". Subparagraph 8(e) clarifies that the term "shares" includes depository receipts thereof. The term "principal class of shares" is defined in subparagraph 8(b) to mean the ordinary or common shares of the company representing the majority of the aggregate voting power and value of the company. If the company does not have a class of ordinary or common shares representing the majority of the aggregate voting power and value of the company, then the "principal class of shares" is that class or any combination of classes of shares that represents, in the aggregate, a majority of the voting power and value of the company. Although in a particular case involving a company with several classes of shares it is conceivable that more than one group of classes could be identified that account for more than 50% of the shares, it is only necessary for one such group to satisfy the requirements of this subparagraph in order for the company to be entitled to benefits. Benefits would not be denied to the company even if a second, non-qualifying, group of shares with more than half of the company's voting power and value could be identified.

A company whose principal class of shares is regularly traded on a recognized stock exchange will nevertheless not be considered a qualified person under subparagraph 2(c) if it has a disproportionate class of shares that is not regularly traded on a recognized stock exchange. The term "disproportionate class of shares" is defined in subparagraph 8(c). A company has a disproportionate class of shares if it has outstanding a class of shares which is subject to terms or other arrangements that entitle the holder to a larger portion of the company's income, profit, or gain in the other Contracting State than that to which the holder would be entitled in the absence of such terms or arrangements. Thus, for example, a company resident in Spain the other Contracting State has a disproportionate class of shares if it has outstanding a class of "tracking stock" that pays dividends based upon a formula that approximates the company's return on its assets employed in the United States.

The following example illustrates this result.

Example. OCo is a corporation resident in Spain. OCo has two classes of shares: Common and Preferred. The Common shares are listed and regularly traded on a Spanish stock exchange controlled by the *Comisión Nacional del Mercado de Valores*. The Preferred shares have no voting rights and are entitled to receive dividends equal in amount to interest payments that OCo receives from unrelated borrowers in the United States. The Preferred shares are owned entirely by a single investor that is a resident of a country with which the United States does not have a tax treaty. The Common shares account for more than 50 percent of the value of OCo and for 100 percent of the voting power. Because the owner of the Preferred shares is entitled to receive payments corresponding to the U.S. source interest income earned by OCo, the Preferred shares are a disproportionate class of shares. Because the Preferred shares are not regularly traded on a recognized stock exchange, OCo will not qualify for benefits under subparagraph (c) of paragraph 2.

The term "regularly traded" is not defined in the Convention. In accordance with paragraph 2 of Article 3 (General Definitions), this term will be defined by reference to the domestic tax laws of the State from which treaty benefits are sought, generally the source State. In the case of the United States, this term is understood to have the meaning it has under Treas. Reg. section 1.884-5(d)(4)(i)(B), relating to the branch tax provisions of the Code. Under these regulations, a class of shares is considered to be "regularly traded" if two requirements are met: trades in the class of shares are made in more than *de minimis* quantities on at least 60 days during the taxable year, and the aggregate number of shares in the class traded during the year is at least 10 percent of the average number of shares outstanding during the year. Sections 1.884-5(d)(4)(i)(A), (ii) and (iii) will not be taken into account for purposes of defining the term "regularly traded" under the Convention.

The regular trading requirement can be met by trading on any recognized exchange or exchanges located in either State. Trading on one or more recognized stock exchanges may be aggregated for purposes of this requirement. Thus, a U.S. company could satisfy the regularly traded requirement through trading, in whole or in part, on any recognized stock exchange. Authorized but unissued shares are not considered for purposes of this test.

The term "primarily traded" is not defined in the Convention. In accordance with paragraph 2 of Article 3 (General Definitions), this term will have the meaning it has under the laws of the State concerning the taxes to which the Convention applies, generally the source State. In the case of the United States, this term is understood to have the meaning it has under Treas. Reg. 1.884-5(d)(3), relating to the branch tax provisions of the Code. Accordingly, stock of a corporation is "primarily traded" if the number of shares in the company's principal class of shares that are traded during the taxable year on all recognized stock exchanges in the Contracting State of which the company is a resident exceeds the number of shares in the company's principal class of shares that are traded during that year on established securities markets in any other single foreign country.

A company whose principal class of shares is regularly traded on a recognized exchange but cannot meet the primarily traded test may claim treaty benefits if its primary place of management and control is in its country of residence. This test is distinct from the "place of effective management" test which is used in the OECD Model and by many other countries to establish residence. In some cases, the place of effective management test has been interpreted to mean the place where the board of directors meets. By contrast, the primary place of management and control test looks to where day-to-day responsibility for the management of the company (and its subsidiaries) is exercised. The company's primary place of management and control will be located in the State in which the company is a resident only if the executive officers and senior management employees exercise day-to-day responsibility for more of the strategic, financial and operational policy decision making for the company (including direct and indirect subsidiaries) in that State than in the other State or any third state, and the staff that support the management in making those decisions are also based in that State. Thus, the test looks to the overall activities of the relevant persons to see where those activities are conducted. In most cases, it will be a necessary, but not a sufficient, condition that the headquarters of the company (that is, the place at which the CEO and other top executives normally are based) be located in the Contracting State of which the company is a resident.

To apply the test, it will be necessary to determine which persons are to be considered "executive officers and senior management employees". In most cases, it will not be necessary to look beyond the executives who are members of the Board of Directors (the "inside directors") in the case of a U.S. company. That will not always be the case, however; in fact, the relevant persons may be employees of subsidiaries if those persons make the strategic, financial and operational policy decisions. Moreover, it would be necessary to take into account any special voting arrangements that result in certain board members making certain decisions without the participation of other board members.

Subsidiaries of Publicly-Traded Corporations -- Subparagraph 2(c)(ii)

A company resident in a Contracting State is entitled to all the benefits of the Convention under clause (ii) of subparagraph (c) of paragraph 2 if five or fewer publicly traded companies described in clause (i) are the direct or indirect owners of at least 50 percent of the aggregate vote and value of the company's shares (and at least 50 percent of any disproportionate class of shares). If the publicly-traded companies are indirect owners, however, each of the intermediate companies must be a resident of one of the Contracting States.

Thus, for example, a company that is a resident of Spain, all the shares of which are owned by another company that is a resident of Spain, would qualify for benefits under the Convention if the principal class of shares (and any disproportionate classes of shares) of the parent company are regularly and primarily traded on a recognized stock exchange in Spain (or within the European Union). However, such a subsidiary would not qualify for benefits under clause (ii) if the publicly traded parent company were a resident of a third state, for example, and not a resident of the United States or Spain. Furthermore, if a parent company in Spain indirectly owned the bottom-tier company through a chain of subsidiaries, each such subsidiary in the chain, as an intermediate owner, must be a resident of the United States or Spain in order for the subsidiary to meet the test in clause (ii).

Tax Exempt Organizations -- Subparagraph 2(d)

Subparagraph 2(d) set forth a limitation on benefits rule for persons referred to in paragraph 4 of the Memorandum of Understanding, which provides that the United States and Spain follow the positions described in paragraph 8.6 of the Commentary to Article 4 (Resident) of the OECD Model. Under clause (i) of subparagraph 2(d), a tax-exempt organization other than a pension fund automatically shall be considered a qualified person without regard to the residence of its beneficiaries or members. Entities qualifying under this rule generally are those that are exempt from tax in their State of residence and that are organized and operated exclusively to fulfill religious, charitable, scientific, artistic, cultural, or educational purposes.

Clause (ii) of paragraph 2(d), sets forth a rule to determine when pension funds described in subparagraph 1(j) of Article 3 (General Definitions) will be considered qualified persons. Clause (A) provides that pension funds described in clauses (i) and (ii)(A) of subparagraph 1(j) of Article 3 will be considered qualified persons if more than fifty percent of the beneficiaries, members or participants of the organization are individuals resident in either Contracting State. For purposes of this provision, the term "beneficiaries" should be understood to refer to the persons receiving benefits from the organization. Pension funds described in clause (ii)(B) of subparagraph 1(j) will be qualified persons if all of the persons for which such pension fund earns income satisfy the requirements of clause (A) of subparagraph 2(d).

Ownership/Base Erosion -- Subparagraph 2(e)

Subparagraph 2(e) provides an additional method to qualify for treaty benefits that applies to any form of legal entity that is a resident of a Contracting State. The test provided in subparagraph (e), the so-called ownership and base erosion test, is a two-part test. Both prongs of the test must be satisfied for the resident to be entitled to treaty benefits under subparagraph 2(e).

The ownership prong of the test, under clause (i), requires that 50 percent or more of each class of shares or other beneficial interests in the person is owned, directly or indirectly, on at least half the days of the person's taxable year by persons who are residents of the Contracting State of which that person is a resident and that are themselves entitled to treaty benefits under subparagraphs (a), (b), (d) or clause (i) of subparagraph (c) of paragraph 2. In the case of indirect owners, however, each of the intermediate owners must be a resident of that Contracting State.

Trusts may be entitled to benefits under this provision if they are treated as residents under Article 4 (Residence) and they otherwise satisfy the requirements of this subparagraph. For purposes of this subparagraph, the beneficial interests in a trust will be considered to be owned by its beneficiaries in proportion to each beneficiary's actuarial interest in the trust. The interest of a remainder beneficiary will be equal to 100 percent less the aggregate percentages held by income beneficiaries. A beneficiary's interest in a trust will not be considered to be owned by a person entitled to benefits under the other provisions of paragraph 2 if it is not possible to determine the beneficiary's actuarial interest. Consequently, if it is not possible to determine the actuarial interest of the beneficiaries in a trust, the ownership test under clause i) cannot be satisfied, unless all possible beneficiaries are persons entitled to benefits under the other subparagraphs of paragraph 2.

The base erosion prong of clause (ii) of subparagraph (e) is satisfied with respect to a person if less than 50 percent of the person's gross income for the taxable year, as determined under the tax law in the person's State of residence, is paid or accrued to persons who are not residents of either Contracting State entitled to benefits under subparagraphs (a), (b), (d) or clause (i) of subparagraph (c) of paragraph 2, in the form of payments deductible for tax purposes in the payer's State of residence. These amounts do not include arm's-length payments in the ordinary course of business for services or tangible property or payments in respect of financial obligations to a bank that is not related to the payer. To the extent they are deductible from the taxable base, trust distributions are deductible payments. However, depreciation and amortization deductions, which do not represent payments or accruals to other persons, are disregarded for this purpose.

Paragraph 3 of New Article 17

Paragraph 3 of new Article 17 sets forth a "derivative benefits" test that is potentially applicable to all treaty benefits, although the test is applied to individual items of income. In general, a derivative benefits test entitles certain companies that are residents of a Contracting State to treaty benefits if the owner of the company would have been entitled to the same benefit had the income in question flowed directly to that owner. To qualify under this paragraph, the company must meet an ownership test and a base erosion test.

Subparagraph 3(a) sets forth the ownership test. Under this test, seven or fewer equivalent beneficiaries must own shares representing at least 95 percent of the aggregate voting power and value of the company and at least 50 percent of any disproportionate class of shares. Ownership may be direct or indirect, although in the case of indirect ownership, each intermediate owner must be a resident of a member state of the European Union or any party to the North American Free Trade Agreement.

The term "equivalent beneficiary" is defined in subparagraph 8(g). This definition may be met in two alternative ways.

Under the first alternative, a person may be an equivalent beneficiary because it is entitled to equivalent benefits under a tax treaty between the country of source and the country in which the person is a resident. This alternative has two requirements.

The first requirement as set forth in clause (i) of subparagraph 8(g) is that the person must be a resident of a member state of the European Union or of a party to the North American Free Trade Agreement (collectively, "qualifying States"). In addition, the person must be entitled to all the benefits of a comprehensive tax treaty between the Contracting State from which benefits of the Convention are claimed and a qualifying state under provisions that are analogous to the rules in subparagraphs 2(a), 2(b), 2(c)(i), or 2(d) of this Article. If the treaty in question does not have a comprehensive limitation on benefits article, this requirement is met only if the person would be entitled to treaty benefits under the tests in subparagraphs 2(a), 2(b), 2(c)(i), or 2(d) of this Article if the person were a resident of one of the Contracting States.

Clause (i)(B) of subparagraph 8(g) requires that with respect to insurance premiums, dividends (including branch profits), interest, and royalties, the person must be entitled to a rate of tax that is at least as low as the tax rate that would apply under the Convention to such income. Thus, the rates to be compared are: (1) the rate of tax that the source State would have imposed if a qualified resident of the other Contracting State was the beneficial owner of the income; and (2) the rate of tax that the source State would have imposed if the third state resident had received the income directly from the source State.

Subparagraph 8(g) provides a special rule to take account of the fact that withholding taxes on many inter-company dividends, interest and royalties are exempt within the European Union by reason of various EU directives, rather than by tax treaty. If a U.S. company is owned by a company resident in a member state of the European Union that would have qualified for an exemption from withholding tax if it had received the income directly and receives such payments from a Spanish company, the parent company will be treated as an equivalent beneficiary. This rule is necessary because many European Union member countries have not re-negotiated their tax treaties to reflect the exemptions available under the directives.

The requirement that a person be entitled to "all the benefits" of a comprehensive tax treaty eliminates those persons that qualify for benefits with respect to only certain types of income. Accordingly, the fact that a French parent of a Spanish company is engaged in the active conduct of a trade or business in France and therefore would be entitled to the benefits of the U.S.-France treaty if it received dividends directly from a U.S. subsidiary of the Spanish company will not qualify such French company as an equivalent beneficiary. Further, the French company cannot be an equivalent beneficiary if it qualifies for benefits only with respect to certain income as a result of a "derivative benefits" provision in the U.S.-France treaty. However, because such French company is a resident of a qualifying state, it would be possible to look through the French company to its parent company to determine whether the parent company is an equivalent beneficiary.

The second alternative for satisfying the "equivalent beneficiary" test is available only to residents of one of the two Contracting States. U.S. or Spanish residents who are eligible for treaty benefits by reason of subparagraphs 2(a), 2(b), 2(c)(i), or 2(d) are equivalent beneficiaries for purposes of the relevant tests in this Article. Thus, a Spanish individual will be an equivalent beneficiary without regard to whether the individual would have been entitled to receive the same benefits if it received the income directly. A resident of a third country cannot qualify for treaty benefits under these provisions by reason of those paragraphs or any other rule of the treaty, and therefore does not qualify as an equivalent beneficiary under this alternative. Thus, a resident of a third country can be an equivalent beneficiary only if it would have been entitled to equivalent benefits had it received the income directly.

The second alternative was included in order to clarify that ownership by certain residents of a Contracting State would not disqualify a U.S. or Spanish company under this paragraph. Thus, for example, if 90 percent of a Spanish company is owned by five companies that are resident in member states of the European Union who satisfy the requirements of subparagraph 8(g)(i), and 10 percent of the Spanish company is owned by a U.S. or Spanish individual, then the Spanish company still can satisfy the requirements of subparagraph 3(a).

Subparagraph 3(b) sets forth the base erosion test. A company meets this base erosion test if less than 50 percent of its gross income (as determined in the company's State of residence) for the taxable period is paid or accrued, directly or indirectly, to a person or persons who are not equivalent beneficiaries in the form of payments deductible for tax purposes in company's State of residence. These deductible payments do not include arm's-length payments in the ordinary course of business for services or tangible property or payments in respect of financial obligations to a bank that is not related to the payor. This test is qualitatively the same as the base erosion test in subparagraph 2(e)(ii), except that the test in paragraph 3(b) focuses on base-eroding payments to persons who are not equivalent beneficiaries.

Paragraph 4 of New Article 17

Paragraph 4 of new Article 17 sets forth an alternative test under which a resident of a Contracting State may receive treaty benefits with respect to certain items of income that are connected to an active trade or business conducted in its State of residence. A resident of a Contracting State may qualify for benefits under paragraph 4 whether or not it also qualifies under paragraph 2.

Subparagraph 4(a) sets forth the general rule that a resident of a Contracting State engaged in the active conduct of a trade or business in that State may obtain the benefits of the Convention with respect to an item of income derived in the other Contracting State. The item of income, however, must be derived in connection with or incidental to that trade or business.

The term "trade or business" is not defined in the Convention. Pursuant to paragraph 2 of Article 3 (General Definitions), when determining whether a resident of

Spain is entitled to the benefits of the Convention under paragraph 3 of this Article with respect to an item of income derived from sources within the United States, the United States will ascribe to this term the meaning that it has under the law of the United States. Accordingly, the U.S. competent authority will refer to the regulations issued under Code section 367(a) for the definition of the term "trade or business." In general, therefore, a trade or business will be considered to be a specific unified group of activities that constitutes or could constitute an independent economic enterprise carried on for profit. Furthermore, a corporation generally will be considered to carry on a trade or business only if the officers and employees of the corporation conduct substantial managerial and operational activities.

The business of making or managing investments for the resident's own account will be considered to be a trade or business only when part of banking, insurance or securities activities conducted by a bank, an insurance company, or a registered securities dealer respectively. Such activities conducted by a person other than a bank, insurance company or registered securities dealer will not be considered to be the conduct of an active trade or business, nor would they be considered to be the conduct of an active trade or business if conducted by a bank, insurance company or registered securities dealer but not as part of the company's banking, insurance or dealer business. Because a headquarters operation is in the business of managing investments, a company that functions solely as a headquarters company will not be considered to be engaged in an active trade or business for purposes of paragraph 4.

An item of income is derived in connection with a trade or business if the income-producing activity in the State of source is a line of business that "forms a part of" or is "complementary" to the trade or business conducted in the State of residence by the income recipient.

A business activity generally will be considered to form part of a business activity conducted in the State of source if the two activities involve the design, manufacture or sale of the same products or type of products, or the provision of similar services. The line of business in the State of residence may be upstream, downstream, or parallel to the activity conducted in the State of source. Thus, the line of business may provide inputs for a manufacturing process that occurs in the State of source, may sell the output of that manufacturing process, or simply may sell the same sorts of products that are being sold by the trade or business carried on in the State of source.

Example 1. USCo is a corporation resident in the United States. USCo is engaged in an active manufacturing business in the United States. USCo owns 100 percent of the shares of FCo, a corporation resident in Spain. FCo distributes USCo products in Spain. Since the business activities conducted by the two corporations involve the same products, FCo's distribution business is considered to form a part of USCo's manufacturing business.

Example 2. The facts are the same as in Example 1, except that USCo does not manufacture. Rather, USCo operates a large research and development facility in the United States that licenses intellectual property to affiliates worldwide, including FCo.

FCo and other USCo affiliates then manufacture and market the USCo-designed products in their respective markets. Since the activities conducted by FCo and USCo involve the same product lines, these activities are considered to form a part of the same trade or business.

For two activities to be considered to be "complementary," the activities need not relate to the same types of products or services, but they should be part of the same overall industry and be related in the sense that the success or failure of one activity will tend to result in success or failure for the other. Where more than one trade or business is conducted in the State of source and only one of the trades or businesses forms a part of or is complementary to a trade or business conducted in the State of residence, it is necessary to identify the trade or business to which an item of income is attributable. Royalties generally will be considered to be derived in connection with the trade or business to which the underlying intangible property is attributable. Dividends will be deemed to be derived first out of earnings and profits of the treaty-benefited trade or business, and then out of other earnings and profits. Interest income may be allocated under any reasonable method consistently applied. A method that conforms to U.S. principles for expense allocation will be considered a reasonable method.

Example 3. Americair is a corporation resident in the United States that operates an international airline. FSub is a wholly-owned subsidiary of Americair resident in Spain. FSub operates a chain of hotels in Spain that are located near airports served by Americair flights. Americair frequently sells tour packages that include air travel to Spain and lodging at FSub hotels. Although both companies are engaged in the active conduct of a trade or business, the businesses of operating a chain of hotels and operating an airline are distinct trades or businesses. Therefore FSub's business does not form a part of Americair's business. However, FSub's business is considered to be complementary to Americair's business because they are part of the same overall industry (travel) and the links between their operations tend to make them interdependent.

Example 4. The facts are the same as in Example 3, except that FSub owns an office building in Spain instead of a hotel chain. No part of Americair's business is conducted through the office building. FSub's business is not considered to form a part of or to be complementary to Americair's business. They are engaged in distinct trades or businesses in separate industries, and there is no economic dependence between the two operations.

Example 5. USFlower is a corporation resident in the United States. USFlower produces and sells flowers in the United States and other countries. USFlower owns all the shares of ForHolding, a corporation resident in Spain. ForHolding is a holding company that is not engaged in a trade or business. ForHolding owns all the shares of three corporations that are resident in Spain: ForFlower, ForLawn, and ForFish. ForFlower distributes USFlower flowers under the USFlower trademark in Spain. ForLawn markets a line of lawn care products in Spain under the USFlower trademark. In addition to being sold under the same trademark, ForLawn and ForFlower products are sold in the same stores and sales of each company's products tend to generate increased sales of the other's products. ForFish imports fish from the United States and distributes

34

it to fish wholesalers in Spain. For purposes of paragraph 3, the business of ForFlower forms a part of the business of USFlower, the business of ForLawn is complementary to the business of USFlower, and the business of ForFish is neither part of nor complementary to that of USFlower.

An item of income derived from the State of source is "incidental to" the trade or business carried on in the State of residence if production of the item facilitates the conduct of the trade or business in the State of residence. An example of incidental income is the temporary investment of working capital of a person in the State of residence in securities issued by persons in the State of source.

Subparagraph (b) of paragraph 4 states a further condition to the general rule in subparagraph (a) in cases where the trade or business generating the item of income in question is carried on either by the person deriving the income or by any associated enterprises. Subparagraph (b) states that the trade or business carried on in the State of residence, under these circumstances, must be substantial in relation to the activity in the State of source. The substantiality requirement is intended to prevent a narrow case of treaty-shopping abuses in which a company attempts to qualify for benefits by engaging in *de minimis* connected business activities in the treaty country in which it is resident (*i.e.*, activities that have little economic cost or effect with respect to the company business as a whole). Paragraph 5 of the Memorandum of Understanding sets forth the understanding of the Contracting States that a person shall be deemed to be related to another person if either person participates directly or indirectly in the management, control or capital of the other, or the same persons participate directly or indirectly in the management, control or capital of both.

The determination of substantiality is made based upon all the facts and circumstances and takes into account the comparative sizes of the trades or businesses in each Contracting State the nature of the activities performed in each Contracting State, and the relative contributions made to that trade or business in each Contracting State. In any case, in making each determination or comparison, due regard will be given to the relative sizes of the economies in the two Contracting States.

The determination in subparagraph (b) also is made separately for each item of income derived from the State of source. It therefore is possible that a person would be entitled to the benefits of the Convention with respect to one item of income but not with respect to another. If a resident of a Contracting State is entitled to treaty benefits with respect to a particular item of income under paragraph 4, the resident is entitled to all benefits of the Convention insofar as they affect the taxation of that item of income in the State of source.

The application of the substantiality requirement only to income from related parties focuses only on potential abuse cases, and does not hamper certain other kinds of non-abusive activities, even though the income recipient resident in a Contracting State may be very small in relation to the entity generating income in the other Contracting State. For example, if a small U.S. research firm develops a process that it licenses to a very large, unrelated, pharmaceutical manufacturer in Spain, the size of the U.S. research firm would not have to be tested against the size of the manufacturer. Similarly, a small U.S. bank that makes a loan to a very large unrelated company operating a business in Spain would not have to pass a substantiality test to receive treaty benefits under paragraph 4.

Subparagraph (c) of paragraph 3 provides special attribution rules for purposes of applying the substantive rules of subparagraphs (a) and (b). Thus, these rules apply for purposes of determining whether a person meets the requirement in subparagraph (a) that it be engaged in the active conduct of a trade or business and that the item of income is derived in connection with that active trade or business, and for making the comparison required by the "substantiality" requirement in subparagraph (b). Subparagraph (c) attributes to a person activities conducted by persons "connected" to such person. A person ("X") is connected to another person ("Y") if X possesses 50 percent or more of the beneficial interest in Y (or if Y possesses 50 percent or more of the beneficial interest in X). For this purpose, X is connected to a company if X owns shares representing fifty percent or more of the aggregate voting power and value of the company or fifty percent or more of the beneficial equity interest in the company. X also is connected to Y if a third person possesses fifty percent or more of the beneficial interest in both X and Y. For this purpose, if X or Y is a company, the threshold relationship with respect to such company or companies is fifty percent or more of the aggregate voting power and value or fifty percent or more of the beneficial equity interest. Finally, X is connected to Y if, based upon all the facts and circumstances, X controls Y, Y controls X, or X and Y are controlled by the same person or persons.

Paragraph 5 of Article 17

Paragraph 5 of new Article 17 provides that a resident of one of the Contracting States is entitled to all the benefits of the Convention if that person functions as a recognized headquarters company for a multinational corporate group. The provisions of this paragraph are consistent with the other U.S. tax treaties where this provision has been adopted. For this purpose, the multinational corporate group includes all corporations that the headquarters company supervises, and excludes affiliated corporations not supervised by the headquarters company. The headquarters company does not have to own shares in the companies that it supervises. In order to be considered a headquarters company, the person must meet several requirements that are enumerated in paragraph 5. These requirements are discussed below.

Overall Supervision and Administration

Subparagraph 5(a) provides that the person must provide a substantial portion of the overall supervision and administration of the group. This activity may include group financing, but group financing may not be the principal activity of the person functioning as the headquarters company. A person only will be considered to engage in supervision and administration if it engages in a number of the following activities: group financing, pricing, marketing, internal auditing, internal communications, and management. Other activities also could be part of the function of supervision and administration.

In determining whether a "substantial portion" of the overall supervision and administration of the group is provided by the headquarters company, its headquarters-related activities must be substantial in relation to the same activities for the same group performed by other entities. Subparagraph 5(a) does not require that the group that is supervised include persons in the other State. However, it is anticipated that in most cases the group will include such persons, due to the requirement in subparagraph 5(g), discussed below, that the income derived in the other Contracting State by the headquarters company be derived in connection with or be incidental to an active trade or business supervised by the headquarters company.

Active Trade or Business

Subparagraph 5(b) is the first of several requirements intended to ensure that the relevant group is truly "multinational." This subparagraph provides that the corporate group supervised by the headquarters company must consist of corporations resident in, and engaged in active trades or businesses in, at least five countries. Furthermore, at least five countries must each contribute substantially to the income generated by the group, as the rule requires that the business activities carried on in each of the five countries (or groupings of countries) generate at least 10 percent of the gross income of the group. For purposes of the 10 percent gross income requirement, the income from multiple countries may be aggregated into non-overlapping groupings, as long as there are at least five individual countries or groupings that each satisfies the 10 percent requirement. If the gross income requirement under this subparagraph is not met for a taxable year, the taxpayer may satisfy this requirement by applying the 10 percent gross income test to the average of the gross incomes for the four years preceding the taxable year.

Example. SHQ is a corporation resident in Spain. SHQ functions as a headquarters company for a group of companies. These companies are resident in the United States, Canada, New Zealand, the United Kingdom, Malaysia, the Philippines, Singapore, and Indonesia. The gross income generated by each of these companies for 2012 and 2013 is as follows:

Country	2012	2013
United States	$40	$45
Canada	$25	$15
New Zealand	$10	$20
United Kingdom	$30	$35
Malaysia	$10	$12
Philippines	$7	$10
Singapore	$10	$8
Indonesia	$5	$10
Total	$137	$155

For 2012, 10 percent of the gross income of this group is equal to $13.70. Only the United States, Canada, and the United Kingdom satisfy this requirement for that year. The other countries may be aggregated to meet this requirement. Because New Zealand

and Malaysia have a total gross income of $20, and the Philippines, Singapore, and Indonesia have a total gross income of $22, these two groupings of countries may be treated as the fourth and fifth members of the group for purposes of subparagraph 5(b).

In the following year, 10 percent of the gross income is $15.50. Only the United States, New Zealand, and the United Kingdom satisfy this requirement. Because Canada and Malaysia have a total gross income of $27, and the Philippines, Singapore, and Indonesia have a total gross income of $28, these two groupings of countries may be treated as the fourth and fifth members of the group for purposes of subparagraph 5(b). The fact that Canada replaced New Zealand in a group is not relevant for this purpose. The composition of the grouping may change from year to year.

Single Country Limitation

Subparagraph 5(c) provides that the business activities carried on in any one country other than the headquarters company's State of residence must generate less than 50 percent of the gross income of the group. If the gross income requirement under this subparagraph is not met for a taxable year, the taxpayer may satisfy this requirement by applying the 50 percent gross income test to the average of the gross incomes for the four years preceding the taxable year. The following example illustrates the application of this clause.

Example. SHQ is a corporation resident in Spain. SHQ functions as a headquarters company for a group of companies. SHQ derives dividend income from a United States subsidiary in the 2008 taxable year. The state of residence of each of these companies, the situs of their activities and the amounts of gross income attributable to each for the years 2008 through 2012 are set forth below.

Country	Situs	2012	2011	2010	2009	2008
United States	U.S.	$100	$100	$95	$90	$85
Mexico	U.S.	$10	$8	$5	$0	$0
Canada	U.S.	$20	$18	$16	$15	$12
United Kingdom	U.K	$30	$32	$30	$28	$27
New Zealand	N.Z.	$35	$42	$38	$36	$35
Japan	Japan	$35	$32	$30	$30	$28
Singapore	Singapore	$30	$25	$24	$22	$20
Total		$260	$257	$238	$221	$207

Because the United States' total gross income of $130 in 2012 is not less than 50 percent of the gross income of the group, subparagraph 5(c) is not satisfied with respect to dividends derived in 2012. However, the United States' average gross income for the preceding four years may be used in lieu of the preceding year's average. The United States' average gross income for the years 2008-11 is $111.00 ($444/4). The group's total average gross income for these years is $230.75 ($923/4). Because $111 represents

48.1 percent of the group's average gross income for the years 2008 through 2011, the requirement under subparagraph 5(c) is satisfied.

Other State Gross Income Limitation

Subparagraph 5(d) provides that no more than 25 percent of the headquarters company's gross income may be derived from the other Contracting State. Thus, if the headquarters company's gross income for the taxable year is $200, no more than $50 of this amount may be derived from the other Contracting State. If the gross income requirement under this subparagraph is not met for a taxable year, the taxpayer may satisfy this requirement by applying the 25 percent gross income test to the average of the gross incomes for the four years preceding the taxable year.

Independent Discretionary Authority

Subparagraph 5(e) requires that the headquarters company have and exercise independent discretionary authority to carry out the functions referred to in subparagraph 5(a). Thus, if the headquarters company was nominally responsible for group financing, pricing, marketing and other management functions, but merely implemented instructions received from another entity, the headquarters company would not be considered to have and exercise independent discretionary authority with respect to these functions. This determination is made individually for each function. For instance, a headquarters company could be nominally responsible for group financing, pricing, marketing and internal auditing functions, but another entity could be actually directing the headquarters company as to the group financing function. In such a case, the headquarters company would not be deemed to have independent discretionary authority for group financing, but it might have such authority for the other functions. Functions for which the headquarters company does not have and exercise independent discretionary authority are considered to be conducted by an entity other than the headquarters company for purposes of subparagraph 5(a).

Income Taxation Rules

Subparagraph 2(f) requires that the headquarters company be subject to the generally applicable income taxation rules in its country of residence. This reference should be understood to mean that the company must be subject to the income taxation rules to which a company engaged in the active conduct of a trade or business would be subject. Thus, if one of the Contracting States has or introduces special taxation legislation that imposes a lower rate of income tax on headquarters companies than is imposed on companies engaged in the active conduct of a trade or business, or provides for an artificially low taxable base for such companies, a headquarters company subject to these rules is not entitled to the benefits of the Convention under paragraph 5.

In Connection With or Incidental to Trade or Business

Subparagraph 5(g) requires that the income derived in the other Contracting State be derived in connection with or be incidental to the active business activities referred to subparagraph 5(b). This determination is made under the principles set forth in paragraph 3. For instance, assume that a Spanish company satisfies the other requirements in paragraph 5 and acts as a headquarters company for a group that includes a U.S. corporation. If the group is engaged in the design and manufacture of computer software, but the U.S. corporation is also engaged in the design and manufacture of photocopying machines, the income that the Spanish company derives from the United States would have to be derived in connection with or be incidental to the income generated by the computer business in order to be entitled to the benefits of the Convention under paragraph 5. Interest income received from the U.S. corporation also would be entitled to the benefits of the Convention under this subparagraph as long as the interest was attributable to the computer business supervised by the headquarters company. Interest income derived from an unrelated party would normally not, however, satisfy the requirements of this clause.

Paragraph 6 of Article 17

Paragraph 6 of new Article 17 deals with the treatment of income in the context of a so-called "triangular case." The term "triangular case" refers to the use of a structure like the one described in the following paragraph by a resident of the other Contracting State to earn income from the United States:

A resident of Spain, who would, absent paragraph 6, qualify for benefits under one or more of the provisions of this Article, sets up a permanent establishment in a third state that imposes a low or zero rate of tax on the income of the permanent establishment. The resident of Spain lends funds into the United States through the permanent establishment. The permanent establishment, despite its third-jurisdiction location, is an integral part of the resident of Spain. Therefore, the income that it earns on those loans, absent the provisions of paragraph 6, is entitled to exemption from U.S. withholding tax under the Convention. Under a current income tax treaty between Spain and the host jurisdiction of the permanent establishment, the income of the permanent establishment is exempt from tax by Spain (alternatively, Spain may choose to exempt the income of the permanent establishment from income tax). Thus, the interest income, absent paragraph 6, would be exempt from U.S. tax, subject to little or no tax in the host jurisdiction of the permanent establishment, and exempt from tax in Spain.

Paragraph 6 provides that the tax benefits that would otherwise apply under the Convention will not apply to any item of income if the combined aggregate effective tax rate in the residence State and the third state is less than 60 percent of the general rate of company tax applicable in the residence State. In the case of dividends, interest and royalties to which this paragraph applies, the withholding tax rates under the Convention are replaced with a 15 percent withholding tax. Any other income to which the provisions of paragraph 6 apply is subject to tax under the domestic law of the source State, notwithstanding any other provisions of the Convention.

In general, the principles employed under Code section 954(b)(4) will be employed to determine whether the profits are subject to an effective rate of taxation that is above the specified threshold.

Notwithstanding the level of tax on interest and royalty income of the permanent establishment, paragraph 6 will not apply under certain circumstances. In the case of royalties, paragraph 6 will not apply if the royalties are received as compensation for the use of, or the right to use, intangible property produced or developed by the permanent establishment itself. In the case of any other income, paragraph 6 will not apply if that income is derived in connection with, or is incidental to, the active conduct of a trade or business carried on by the permanent establishment in the third state. The business of making, managing or simply holding investments is not considered to be an active trade or business, unless these are securities activities carried on by a registered securities dealer.

Paragraph 6 applies reciprocally. However, the United States does not exempt the profits of a third-jurisdiction permanent establishment of a U.S. resident from U.S. tax, either by statute or by treaty.

Paragraph 7 of New Article 17

Paragraph 7 of new Article 17 provides that a resident of one of the States that is not entitled to the benefits of the Convention as a result of paragraphs 1 through 5 may be granted benefits under the Convention at the discretion of the competent authority of the State from which benefits in certain circumstances. Such competent authority shall make the determination of whether the granting of benefits would be justified based on an evaluation of the extent to which such resident satisfies the requirements of paragraphs 2, 3, 4 or 5. Such competent authority shall also consider the opinion, if any of the competent authority of the other Contracting State as to whether under the circumstances it would be appropriate to grant such benefits.

A competent authority may grant all of the benefits of the Convention to the taxpayer making the request, or it may grant only certain benefits. For instance, it may grant benefits only with respect to a particular item of income in a manner similar to paragraph 3. Further, the competent authority may establish conditions, such as setting time limits on the duration of any relief granted.

For purposes of implementing paragraph 7, a taxpayer will be permitted to present his case to the relevant competent authority for an advance determination based on the facts. In these circumstances, it is also expected that, if the competent authority determines that benefits are to be allowed, they will be allowed retroactively to the time of entry into force of the relevant treaty provision or the establishment of the structure in question, whichever is later.

Finally, there may be cases in which a resident of a Contracting State may apply for discretionary relief to the competent authority of his State of residence. This would arise, for example, if the benefit it is claiming is provided by the residence country, and not by the source country. So, for example, if a company that is a resident of the United States would like to claim the benefit of treaty-based relief from double taxation under Article 24 (Relief from Double Taxation), but it does not meet any of the objective tests of paragraphs 2 through 5, it may apply to the U.S. competent authority for discretionary relief.

Paragraph 8 of New Article 17

Paragraph 8 of new Article 17 defines several key terms for purposes of Article 17. Each of the defined terms is discussed above in the context in which it is used.

Article X

Article X of the Protocol amends Article 20 (Pensions, Annuities, Alimony and Child Support) of the existing Convention by adding a new paragraph 5.

New Paragraph 5 of Article 20

New paragraph 5 provides that, if a resident of a Contracting State participates in a pension fund established in the other Contracting State, the State of residence will not tax the income of the pension fund with respect to that resident until a distribution is made from the pension fund. Thus, for example, if a U.S. citizen contributes to a U.S. qualified plan while working in the United States and then establishes residence in Spain, paragraph 5 prevents Spain from taxing currently the plan's earnings and accretions with respect to that individual. When the resident receives a distribution from the pension fund, that distribution may be subject to tax in the State of residence, subject to paragraph 1 of Article 20.

Article XI

Article XI of the Protocol replaces paragraph 3 of Article 25 (Non-Discrimination) of the existing Convention in order to conform to changes made by the deletion of Article 14 and the changes made to Article 10 dealing with the taxation of branch profits tax. It clarifies that nothing in Article 25 should be construed as preventing either Contracting State from imposing a tax described in paragraph 8 of Article 10 (Dividends) as revised by Article IV.

Article XII

Article XII of the Protocol makes amendments to Article 26 (Mutual Agreement Procedure) of the existing Convention, which deals with the mutual agreement procedure. In particular, Article XII of the Protocol incorporates into Article 26 rules that provide for mandatory binding arbitration to resolve certain cases that the competent authorities of the Contracting States have been unable to resolve after a reasonable amount of time.

New Paragraph 5 of Article 26

New paragraph 5 provides that a case shall be resolved through mandatory binding arbitration when a "concerned person" as defined in subparagraph 6(a) has presented a case to the competent authority of either Contracting State on the basis that the actions of one or both of the Contracting States have resulted for that person in taxation not in accordance with the provisions of the Convention, and the competent authorities of the Contracting States have not been able to reach an agreement to resolve the case, and if the conditions specified in this paragraph and in paragraph 6 are satisfied. The mandatory binding arbitration provision is an extension of (as opposed to an alternative to) the interaction between the competent authorities as provided in the mutual agreement procedure. Accordingly, only cases that have first been negotiated by the competent authorities pursuant to Article 26 shall be eligible for arbitration.

An initial condition set forth in paragraph 5 is that a concerned person has presented a case to the competent authority of either Contracting State on the basis that the actions of one or both of the Contracting States have resulted for that person in taxation not in accordance with the provisions of the Convention. Such taxation should be considered to have resulted from the actions of one or both of the Contracting States as soon as, for example, tax has been paid, assessed, or otherwise determined, or even in cases where the taxpayer is officially notified by the tax authorities that they intend to tax him on a certain element of income. As provided in paragraph 18 of the Protocol of 1990 as revised by Article XIV of the Protocol, in the case of the United States, such notification would take the form of a notice of proposed adjustment, and in Spain, such notification would include a notification of the Administrative Act of Assessment.

The additional conditions that must be satisfied before a case may be resolved through arbitration are set forth in subparagraphs 5(a) through 5(e). Subparagraph 5(a) provides that tax returns must be filed with at least one of the Contracting States with respect to the taxable years at issue in the case. Subparagraph 5(b) provides that the case may not be a case that the competent authorities have mutually agreed before the date on which arbitration proceedings would otherwise have begun, is not suitable for determination by arbitration. Subparagraph 5(c) provides that an unresolved case shall not be submitted to arbitration if a decision on such case has already been rendered by a court or administrative tribunal of either Contracting State. Subparagraph 5(d) provides that the case must not involve a determination under paragraph 3 of Article 4 (Residence) dealing with dual resident entities. Finally, subparagraph 5(e) provides that the provisions of subparagraph 6(c), described below, which sets forth the rule governing the date on which an arbitration proceeding shall commence, must be satisfied.

New paragraph 6 of Article 26

New paragraph 6 sets forth additional rules and definitions to be used in applying the arbitration provisions. Subparagraph 6(a) defines the term "concerned person" as the person that brought the case to competent authority for consideration under Article 26 and all other persons, if any, whose tax liability to either Contracting State may be directly affected by a mutual agreement arising from that consideration. For example, a concerned person would include a U.S. corporation that brings a transfer pricing case with respect to a transaction entered into with its subsidiary in Spain for resolution to the U.S. competent authority, as well as the subsidiary, which may seek a correlative adjustment as a result of the resolution of the case.

Subparagraph 6(b) defines the term "commencement date" as the earliest date on which the information necessary to undertake substantive consideration for a mutual agreement has been received by the competent authorities of both Contracting States. The competent authority of the United States will be considered to have received the information necessary to undertake substantive consideration for a mutual agreement on the date that it has received the information that must be submitted pursuant to Rev Proc. 2006-54, 2006-2 C.B. 1035,§ 4.05 (or any similarly applicable or successor procedures). The competent authority of Spain will be considered to have received the information necessary to undertake substantive consideration for a mutual agreement on the date it has received the information that must be submitted pursuant to Article 6 of Royal Decree 1794/2008 of November 3 (or any similarly applicable or successor procedures). The information shall not be considered received until both competent authorities have received copies of all materials submitted to either Contracting State by the concerned person(s) in connection with the mutual agreement procedure.

Subparagraph 6(c) provides that an arbitration proceeding shall begin on the latest of four dates: (i) two years from the commencement date of that case (unless both competent authorities have previously agreed to a different date), (ii) the date upon which the present of the case has submitted a written request to a competent authority for a resolution of the case through arbitration, (iii) the earliest date upon which all concerned persons have entered into a confidentiality agreement and the agreements have been received by both competent authorities, or (iv) the date on which all legal actions or suits pending before the courts of either Contracting State concerning any issue involved in the care are suspended or withdrawn (as applicable) under the laws of the Contracting State in which the legal actions or suits are pending.

Clause (i) of this subparagraph permits the competent authorities of the Contracting States to mutually agree to initiate arbitration proceedings on a date other than two years after the commencement date. This could be the case, for instance, if the negotiation of a case between the competent authorities was nearing completion and could be expected to be resolved in an additional short period of time, thus avoiding the need for an arbitration proceeding. As another example, if under paragraphs 5 and 6 arbitration proceedings would be initiated on the same date for a large number of cases, clause (i) would allow the competent authorities of the Contracting States to agree to establish different dates (including accelerated dates) to initiate arbitration proceedings for such cases in order to avoid having multiple arbitration proceedings take place at the same time. Clause (i) requires that the competent authorities of the Contracting States notify the presenter of the case of any such agreements.

Clause (ii) of this subparagraph provides that the presenter of the case must submit a written request to the competent authority for a resolution of the case through arbitration. However, the presenter of the case may not submit such written request prior to the completion of the two year period after the commencement date described in clause (i).

Clause (iii) of this subparagraph requires that all concerned persons and their authorized representatives or agents agree in writing prior to the beginning of an arbitration proceeding not to disclose to any other person any information received during the course of the arbitration proceeding from either Contracting State or the arbitration panel, other than the determination of the panel. A confidentiality agreement may be executed by any concerned person that has the legal authority to bind any other concerned person on the matter. For example, a parent corporation with the legal authority to bind its subsidiary with respect to confidentiality may execute a comprehensive confidentiality agreement on its own behalf and that of its subsidiary.

Clause (iv) of this subparagraph requires that in the event that any issue involved in the case that is potentially subject to arbitration is the subject of any legal actions or suits pending before the courts of either Contracting States, such legal action must be either suspended or withdrawn as applicable under the laws of the Contracting State in which such legal actions or suits are pending.

Subparagraph 6(d) provides that the determination of the arbitration panel shall constitute a resolution by mutual agreement under Article 26 and thus shall be binding on the Contracting States. As is the case with any negotiated resolution between the competent authorities pursuant to the mutual agreement procedure, the presenter of the case preserves the right not to accept the determination of the arbitration panel.

Subparagraph 6(e) provides that for purposes of an arbitration proceeding under paragraphs 5 and 6 of Article 26, the members of the arbitration panel and their staff shall be considered "persons or authorities" to whom information may be disclosed under Article 27 (Exchange of Information and Administrative Assistance) of the Convention as revised by Article XIII.

Subparagraph 6(f) sets forth the confidentiality obligations of the competent authorities of the Contracting States as well as the members of the arbitration panel and their staffs regarding an arbitration proceeding. Subparagraph 6(g) provides that no information relating to an arbitration proceeding (including the arbitration panel's determination) may be disclosed by the competent authorities of the Contracting States, except as permitted by this Convention and the domestic laws of the Contracting States. In addition, all material prepared in the course of, or relating to, an arbitration proceeding shall be considered to be information exchanged between the Contracting States. Subparagraph 6(f) requires that all members of the arbitration panel and their staff make statements in writing not to disclose any information relating to an arbitration proceeding (including the arbitration panel's determination), and to abide by and be subject to the confidentiality and nondisclosure provisions of Article 27 of this Convention and the applicable domestic laws of the Contracting States. In the event those provisions conflict, the most restrictive condition shall apply. These statements from the members of the arbitration panel shall also include confirmation of their appointment to the arbitration panel.

Subparagraph 6(g) sets forth a non-exhaustive list of items related to the time periods and procedures related to conducting an arbitration proceeding that the competent authorities of the Contracting States must agree to in order to ensure the effective and timely implementation of the provisions of paragraph 5 and 6 of Article 26. Such agreement must be consistent with the provisions of paragraphs 5 and 6 of Article 25 and paragraph 21 of the Protocol of 1990 as amended by Article XIV, and shall take the form of published guidance before the date that the first arbitration proceeding commences. Subparagraph 6(g) lists the following items for which the competent authorities of the Contracting States shall agree on time frames and procedures for:

i)   notifying the presenter of the case of any agreements pursuant to either subparagraph 5(b) that the case is not suitable for resolution through arbitration, or clause i) of subparagraph 5(c) to change the date on which an arbitration proceeding could begin;

ii)   obtaining the statements of each concerned person, authorized representative or agent, and member of the arbitration panel (including their staff), in which each such person agrees not to disclose to any other person any information received during the course of the arbitration proceeding from the competent authority of either Contracting State or the arbitration panel, other than the determination of such panel;

iii)   the appointment of the members of the arbitration panel;

iv)   the submission of proposed resolutions, position papers, and reply submissions by the competent authorities of the Contracting States to the arbitration panel;

v)   the submission by the presenter of the case of a paper setting forth the presenter's views and analysis of the case for consideration by the arbitration panel;

vi)   the delivery by the arbitration panel of its determination to the competent authorities of the Contracting States;

vii)   the acceptance or rejection by the presenter of the case of the determination of the arbitration panel; and

vii)   the adoption by the arbitration panel of any additional procedures necessary for the conduct of its business.

Paragraph 6 also provides that the competent authorities of the Contracting States may agree in writing on such other rules, time periods or procedures as may be necessary for the effective and timely implementation of the provisions of paragraphs 5 and 6 of Article 26.

Article XIII

Article XIII of the Protocol replaces Article 27 (Exchange of Information and Administrative Assistance) of the existing Convention. This Article provides for the exchange of information between the competent authorities of the Contracting States. While mutual agreement procedures are addressed in Article 26, exchanges of information for purposes of the mutual agreement procedures are governed by this Article.

Paragraph 1 of New Article 27

The obligation to obtain and provide information to the other Contracting State is set out in paragraph 1 of new Article 27. The information to be exchanged is that which may be is foreseeably relevant for carrying out the provisions of the Convention or the domestic laws of the United States or of the other Contracting State concerning taxes of every kind applied at the national level. This language incorporates the standard of the OECD Model. The Contracting States intend for the phrase "is foreseeably relevant" to be interpreted to permit the exchange of information that "may be relevant" for purposes of 26 U.S.C. Section 7602 of the Code, which authorizes the IRS to examine "any books, papers, records, or other data which *may* be relevant or material." (emphasis added.). In United States v. Arthur Young & Co., 465 U.S. 805, 814 (1984), the Supreme Court stated that the language "may be" reflects Congress's express intention to allow the IRS to obtain "items of even *potential* relevance to an ongoing investigation, without reference to its admissibility." (emphasis in original.). However, the language "may be" would not support a request in which a Contracting State simply asked for information regarding all bank accounts maintained by residents of that Contracting State in the other Contracting State., or even all accounts maintained by its residents with respect to a particular bank. Thus, the language of paragraph 1 is intended to provide for exchange of information in tax matters to the widest extent possible, while clarifying that Contracting States are not at liberty to engage in "fishing expeditions" or otherwise to request information that is unlikely to be relevant to the tax affairs of a given taxpayer.

Consistent with the OECD Model, a request for information does not constitute a "fishing expedition" solely because it does not provide the name or address (or both) of the taxpayer under examination or investigation. In cases where the requesting State does not provide the name or address (or both) of the taxpayer under examination or investigation, the requesting State must provide other information sufficient to identify the taxpayer. Similarly, paragraph 1 does not necessarily require the request to include the name and/or address of the person believed to be in possession of the information.

The standard of "foreseeable relevance" can be met in cases dealing with both one taxpayer (whether identified by name or otherwise) or several taxpayers (whether identified by name or otherwise). Where a Contracting State undertakes an investigation into an ascertainable group or category of persons in accordance with its laws, any request related to the investigation will typically serve the objective of carrying out the domestic tax laws of the requesting State administration or enforcement of its domestic laws and thus will comply with the requirements of paragraph 1, provided it meets the standard of "foreseeable relevance." In such cases, the requesting State should provide, supported by a clear factual basis, a detailed description of the group or category of persons and of the specific facts and circumstances that have led to the request, as well as an explanation of the applicable law and why there is reason to believe that the taxpayers in the group or category of persons for whom information is requested have been non-compliant with that law supported by a clear factual basis. The requesting State should further show that the requested information would assist in determining compliance by the taxpayers in the group or category of persons.

Exchange of information with respect to each State's domestic law is authorized to the extent that taxation under domestic law is not contrary to the Convention. Thus, for example, information may be exchanged under this Article, even if the transaction to which the information relates is a purely domestic transaction in the requesting State and, therefore, the exchange is not made to carry out the Convention. An example of such a case is provided in subparagraph 8(b) of the OECD Commentary: a company resident in one Contracting State and a company resident in the other Contracting State transact business between themselves through a third-country resident company. Neither Contracting State has a treaty with the third state. To enforce their internal laws with respect to transactions of their residents with the third-country company (since there is no relevant treaty in force), the Contracting States may exchange information regarding the prices that their residents paid in their transactions with the third-country resident.

Paragraph 1 clarifies that information may be exchanged that relates to the assessment or collection of, the enforcement or prosecution in respect of, or the determination of appeals in relation to, taxes of every kind imposed by a Contracting State at the national level. Accordingly, the competent authorities may request and provide information for cases under examination or criminal investigation, in collection, on appeals, or under prosecution, and information may be exchanged with respect to U.S. estate and gift taxes. In contrast, paragraph 7, which relates to collection assistance, applies only to those taxes covered for general purposes of the Convention as defined in Article 2 (Taxes Covered).

Information exchange is not restricted by paragraph 1 of Article 1. Accordingly, information may be requested and provided under this Article with respect to persons who are not residents of either Contracting State. For example, if a third-country resident has a permanent establishment in the other Contracting State, and that permanent establishment engages in transactions with a U.S. enterprise, the United States could request information with respect to that permanent establishment, even though the third-country resident is not a resident of either Contracting State. Similarly, if a third-country resident maintains a bank account in the other Contracting State, and the Internal Revenue Service has reason to believe that funds in that account should have been reported for U.S. tax purposes but have not been so reported, information can be requested from the other Contracting State with respect to that person's account, even though that person is not the taxpayer under examination.

Although the term "United States" does not encompass U.S. possessions or territories for most purposes of the Convention, section 7651 of the Code authorizes the Internal Revenue Service to utilize the administrative and enforcement provisions of the Code in the U.S. possessions or territories, including to obtain information pursuant to a proper request made under Article 26. If necessary to obtain requested information, the Internal Revenue Service could issue and enforce an administrative summons to the taxpayer, a tax authority (or other U.S. possession or territory government agency), or a third party located in a U.S. possession or territory.

The final sentence of paragraph 1 provides that the requesting Contracting State may specify the form in which information is to be provided (e.g., authenticated copies of original documents (including books, papers, statements, records, accounts, and writings)). The intention is to ensure that the information may be introduced as evidence in the judicial proceedings of the requesting State. The requested State should, if possible, provide the information in the form requested to the same extent that it can obtain information in that form under its own laws and administrative practices with respect to its own taxes.

Paragraph 2 of New Article 27

Paragraph 2 provides assurances that any information exchanged will be treated as secret, subject to the same disclosure constraints as information obtained under the laws of the requesting State. The confidentiality rules cover communications between the competent authorities (including the letter requesting information) as well as references to exchanged information that may occur in other documents, such as advice by government attorneys to their respective competent authorities. At the same time, it is understood that the requested State can disclose the minimum information contained in a competent authority letter (but not the letter itself) necessary for the requested State to be able to obtain or provide the requested information to the requesting State, without frustrating the efforts of the requesting State. If, however, court proceedings or the like under the domestic laws of the requested State necessitate the disclosure of the competent authority letter itself, the competent authority of the requested State may disclose such a letter unless the requesting State otherwise specifies.

Information received may be disclosed only to persons or authorities, including courts and administrative bodies, involved in the assessment, collection, or administration of, the enforcement or prosecution in respect of, or the determination of appeals in relation to, the taxes referred to in paragraph 1. Under this standard, information may be communicated to the taxpayer or his proxy. The information must be used by these persons only for the purposes mentioned in paragraph 2. Information may also be disclosed to legislative bodies, such as the tax-writing committees of the U.S. Congress and the U.S. Government Accountability Office, engaged in the oversight of the preceding activities. Information received by these bodies must be for use in the performance of their role in overseeing the administration of U.S. tax laws. Information received may be disclosed in public court proceedings or in judicial decisions.

In situations in which the requested State determines that the requesting State does not comply with its duties regarding the confidentiality of the information exchanged under this Article, the requested State may suspend assistance under this Article until such time as proper assurance is given by the requesting State that those duties will indeed be respected. If necessary, the competent authorities may enter into specific arrangements or memoranda of understanding regarding the confidentiality of the information exchanged under this Article.

Paragraph 2 also provides that the competent authority of the Contracting State that receives information under this Article may, with the written consent of the other Contracting State, make that information available to be used for other purposes allowed under the provisions of a mutual legal assistance treaty in force between the Contracting States that allows for the exchange of tax information.

Paragraph 3 of New Article 27

Paragraph 3 of new Article 27 provides that the obligations undertaken in paragraphs 1 and 2 to exchange information do not require a Contracting State to carry out administrative measures that are at variance with the laws or administrative practice of either State. Nor is a Contracting State required to supply information not obtainable under the laws or administrative practice of either State, or to disclose trade secrets or other information, the disclosure of which would be contrary to public policy.

Thus, a requesting State may be denied information from the other State if the information would be obtained pursuant to procedures or measures that are broader than those available in the requesting State. However, the statute of limitations of the Contracting State making the request for information should govern a request for information. Thus, the Contracting State of which the request is made should attempt to obtain the information even if its own statute of limitations has passed. In many cases, relevant information will still exist in the business records of the taxpayer or a third party, even though it is no longer required to be kept for domestic tax purposes.

While paragraph 3 states conditions under which a Contracting State is not obligated to comply with a request from the other Contracting State for information, the requested State is not precluded from providing such information, and may, at its discretion, do so subject to the limitations of its internal law.

Paragraph 4 of New Article 27

Paragraph 4 of new Article 27 provides that when information is requested by a Contracting State in accordance with this Article, the other Contracting State is obligated to obtain the requested information as if the tax in question were the tax of the requested State, even if that State has no direct tax interest in the case to which the request relates.

In the absence of such a paragraph, some taxpayers have argued that subparagraph 3(a) prevents a Contracting State from requesting information from a bank or fiduciary that the Contracting State does not need for its own tax purposes. This paragraph clarifies that paragraph 3 does not impose such a restriction and that a Contracting State is not limited to providing only the information that it already has in its own files.

Paragraph 5 of New Article 27

Paragraph 5 of new Article 27 provides that a Contracting State may not decline to provide information because that information is held by banks, other financial institutions, nominees or persons acting in an agency or fiduciary capacity or because it relates to ownership interests in a person. Thus, paragraph 5 would effectively prevent a Contracting State from relying on paragraph 3 to argue that its domestic bank secrecy laws (or similar legislation relating to disclosure of financial information by financial institutions or intermediaries) override its obligation to provide information under paragraph 1. This paragraph also requires the disclosure of information regarding the beneficial owner of an interest in a person, such as the identity of a beneficial owner of bearer shares.

Subparagraphs 3 (a) and (b) do not permit the requested State to decline a request where paragraph 4 or 5 applies. Paragraph 5 would apply, for instance, in situations in which the requested State's inability to obtain the information was specifically related to the fact that the requested information was believed to be held by a bank or other financial institution. Thus, the application of paragraph 5 includes situations in which the tax authorities' information gathering powers with respect to information held by banks and other financial institutions are subject to different requirements than those that are generally applicable with respect to information held by persons other than banks or other financial institutions. This would, for example, be the case where the tax authorities can only exercise their information gathering powers with respect to information held by banks and other financial institutions in instances where specific information on the taxpayer under examination or investigation is available. This would also be the case where, for example, the use of information gathering measures with respect to information held by banks and other financial institutions requires a higher probability that the information requested is held by the person believed to be in possession of the requested information than the degree of probability required for the use of information gathering measures with respect to information believed to be held by persons other than banks or financial institutions.

Paragraph 6 of New Article 27

Paragraph 6 of new Article 27 provides that the requesting State may specify the form in which information is to be provided (*e.g.*, depositions of witnesses and authenticated copies of original documents). The intention is to ensure that the information may be introduced as evidence in the judicial proceedings of the requesting State. The requested State should, if possible, provide the information in the form requested to the same extent that it can obtain information in that form under its own laws and administrative practices with respect to its own taxes.

Paragraph 7 of New Article 27

Paragraph 7 provides for assistance in collection of taxes to the extent necessary to ensure that treaty benefits are enjoyed only by persons entitled to those benefits under the terms of the Convention. Under paragraph 7, a Contracting State will endeavor to collect on behalf of the other State only those amounts necessary to ensure that any exemption or reduced rate of tax granted under the Convention by that other State is not enjoyed by persons not entitled to those benefits. For example, if the payer of a U.S.-source portfolio dividend receives a Form W-8BEN or other appropriate documentation from the payee, the withholding agent is permitted to withhold at the portfolio dividend rate of 15 percent. If, however, the addressee is merely acting as a nominee on behalf of a third-country resident, paragraph 7 would obligate Spain to withhold and remit to the United States the additional tax that should have been collected by the U.S. withholding agent.

This paragraph also makes clear that the Contracting State asked to collect the tax is not obligated, in the process of providing collection assistance, to carry out administrative measures that are different from the laws or administrative practice of either Contracting State from those used in the collection of its own taxes, or that would be contrary to its sovereignty, security, or public policy.

Paragraph 8 of New Article 27

Paragraph 8 of new Article 27 states that the competent authorities of the Contracting States may develop an agreement concerning the mode of application of the Article. The Article authorizes the competent authorities to exchange information on an automatic basis, on request in relation to a specific case, or spontaneously. It is contemplated that the Contracting States will utilize this authority to engage in all of these forms of information exchange, as appropriate.

The competent authorities may also agree on specific procedures and timetables for the exchange of information. In particular, the competent authorities may agree on minimum thresholds regarding tax at stake or take other measures aimed at ensuring some measure of reciprocity with respect to the overall exchange of information between the Contracting States.

Effective dates and termination in relation to exchange of information

Once the Protocol is in force, the competent authority may seek information under the Protocol with respect to a year prior to the entry into force of the Protocol. In that case, the competent authorities have available to them the full range of information exchange provisions afforded under this Article.

In contrast, if the provisions of new Article 27 were to terminate in accordance with the provisions of Article 30 (Termination) of the existing Convention, it would cease to authorize, as of the date of termination, any exchange of information, even with respect to a year for which the Protocol was in force. In such case, the tax administrations of the two countries would only be able to exchange information to the extent allowed under either domestic law or another international agreement or arrangement.

Article XIV

This Article makes a number of amendments to the Protocol of 1990.

Paragraph 1

Paragraph 1 amends paragraph 5 of the Protocol of 1990 by deleting subparagraph 5(b) and renaming subparagraph 5(c) as subparagraph 5(b). Existing subparagraph 5(b) was deleted because it is no longer necessary, given the inclusion into Article 1 (General Scope) of the Convention of new paragraph 6, pursuant to Article 1 of this Protocol.

Paragraph 2

Paragraph 2 replaces paragraph 7 of the Protocol of 1990. In the case of Spain, new subparagraph 7(a) provides special rules regarding dividend withholding on dividends paid by certain Spanish entities. Clause (i) provides that the 5 percent withholding limitation provided in subparagraph 2(a) of Article 10 (Dividends) shall not apply in the case of dividends paid by an entity regulated under the law 11/2009 of 26th October on *Sociedades Anónimas Cotizadas de Inversión en el Mercado Inmobiliario* (SOCIMI) or successor statutes. Instead, the 15 percent withholding limitation provided in subparagraph 2(b) of Article 10, or the exemption from withholding provided in paragraph 4 of Article 10 for dividends paid to pension funds, as the case may be, shall apply with respect to such dividends, but only if the beneficial owner of the dividends holds, directly or indirectly, capital that represents no more than 10 percent of all of the capital in the SOCIMI. Clause (ii) provides that the 5 percent withholding limitation shall also not apply in the case of dividends paid by a Spanish investment institution regulated under the law 35/2003 of 4th November on *Instituciones de Inversión Colectiva* or successor statutes. Instead, the 15 percent withholding limitation provided in subparagraph 2(b) of Article 10, or the exemption from withholding provided in paragraph 4 of Article 10 for dividends paid to pension funds, as the case may be, shall apply with respect to such dividends.

In the case of the United States, new subparagraph 7(b) imposes limitations on the rate reductions provided by subparagraph 2(a) of revised Article 10 in the case of dividends paid by a regulated investment company (RIC) or a real estate investment trust (REIT). The first sentence of new subparagraph 7(b) provides that dividends paid by a RIC or REIT are not eligible for the 5 percent rate of withholding tax of subparagraph 2(a) of revised Article 10. The second sentence of new subparagraph 7(b) provides that the 15 percent maximum rate of withholding tax of subparagraph 2(b) of revised Article 10 applies to dividends paid by RICs and that the elimination of source-country withholding tax of paragraph 4 of revised Article 10 applies to dividends paid by RICs and beneficially owned by a pension fund.

The third sentence of new subparagraph 7(b) provides that the 15 percent rate of withholding tax also applies to dividends paid by a REIT and that the elimination of source-country withholding tax of paragraph 4 of revised Article 10 applies to dividends paid by REITs and beneficially owned by a pension fund, provided that one of the three following conditions is met. First, the beneficial owner of the dividend is an individual or a pension fund, in either case holding an interest of not more than 10 percent in the REIT. Second, the dividend is paid with respect to a class of stock that is publicly traded and the beneficial owner of the dividend is a person holding an interest of not more than 5 percent of any class of the REIT's shares. Third, the beneficial owner of the dividend holds an interest in the REIT of not more than 10 percent and the REIT is "diversified."

New subparagraph 7(b) provides a definition of the term "diversified." A REIT is diversified if the gross value of no single interest in real property held by the REIT exceeds 10 percent of the gross value of the REIT's total interest in real property. Section 856(e) foreclosure property is not considered an interest in real property, and a REIT holding a partnership interest is treated as owning its proportionate share of any interest in real property held by the partnership.

Paragraph 3

Paragraph 3 replaces paragraph 8 of the Protocol of 1990. New paragraph 8 provides a definition of the term "real estate mortgage investment conduit (REMIC)" for purposes of revised Article 11 (Interest) of the Convention as amended by Article V. The term means an entity that has in effect an election to be treated as a REMIC under Code Section 860D.

Paragraph 4

Paragraph 4 deletes subparagraph 10(c) of the Protocol of 1990 as a conforming change to the amendments made to Article 13 (Capital Gains) of the Convention by Article VII.

Paragraph 5

Paragraph 5 deletes paragraph 11 of the Protocol of 1990 as a conforming change to the deletion of Article 14 (Branch Tax) of the Convention by Article VIII.

Paragraph 6

Paragraph 6 deletes paragraph 12 of the Protocol of 1990. Prior paragraph 12 referred to Commentary on Article 14 (Independent Personal Services) of the 1977 Model Convention for the Avoidance of Double Taxation with Respect to Taxes on

Income and on Capital of the Organisation for Economic Cooperation and Development, and of any guidelines which, for the application of such Article, may be developed in the future. The deletion of prior paragraph 12 ensures that the Contracting States can interpret Article 14 (Independent Personal Services) of the Convention in an ambulatory manner and consistently with the prevailing Commentaries of the OECD Model.

Paragraph 7

Paragraph 7 amends paragraph 13 of the Protocol of 1990. Revised paragraph 13 describes in a non-exhaustive fashion those entities to which clause (ii) of subparagraph 2(d) of revised Article 17 (Limitation on Benefits) as restated by Article IX applies. Because under Spain's current domestic law, a number of the entities described, including pension funds established in Spain, are not exempt from tax, the words "tax exempt" have been deleted from paragraph 13.

Paragraph 8

Paragraph 8 replaces paragraph 18 of the Protocol of 1990. New paragraph 8 defines the term "first notification" for the purposes of applying paragraph 1 of Article 26 (Mutual Agreement Procedure) of the Convention. The term means, in the case of the United States, the Notice of Proposed Adjustment, and in the case of Spain, the Notification of the Administrative Act of Assessment.

With respect to paragraph 5 of Article 26 as amended by Article XII, paragraph 8 clarifies when taxation not in accordance with the Convention shall be considered to have resulted from the actions of one or both of the Contracting States. The Contracting States understand that an action of either Contracting State that has resulted in taxation not in accordance with the provisions of the Convention shall include a Notice of Proposed Adjustment, a Notification of the Administrative Act of Assessment or in the case of taxes at source, a payment or withholding of tax.

Paragraph 9

Paragraph 9 deletes paragraph 19 of the Protocol of 1990. The deletion of prior paragraph 19 permits the Contracting States to interpret Article 27 (Exchange of Information and Administrative Assistance) of the Convention as amended by Article XIII, in an ambulatory manner and consistently with the prevailing Commentaries of the OECD Model.

Paragraph 10

Paragraph 10 adds a new paragraph 21 to the Protocol of 1990. New paragraph 21 sets forth a number of principles related to the implementation of the mandatory binding arbitration rules provided in new paragraphs 5 and 6 of Article 26 (Mutual Agreement Procedure).

New subparagraph 21(a) of the Protocol to 1990 sets forth rules that the competent authorities of the Contracting States shall follow for selecting the members of the arbitration panel. The arbitration panel shall consist of three individual members. The members appointed shall not be employees nor have been employees within the twelve-month period prior to the date on which the arbitration proceeding begins, of the tax administration, the Treasury Department or the Ministry of Finance of the Contracting State which identifies them. Each competent authority of the Contracting States shall select one member of the arbitration panel. The two members of the arbitration panel who have been selected shall select the third member, who shall serve as Chair of the arbitration panel. If the two initial members of the arbitration panel fail to select the third member in the manner and within the time periods prescribed by the competent authorities of the Contracting States pursuant to subparagraph 6(g)(iii) of Article 26 of the Convention, these members shall be dismissed, and each competent authority of the Contracting States shall select a new member of the arbitration panel. The Chair shall not be a national or lawful permanent resident of either Contracting State.

New subparagraph 21(b) of the Protocol of 1990 provides that if at any time before the arbitration panel delivers a determination to the competent authorities certain events occur, notwithstanding the initiation of an arbitration proceeding, the arbitration proceeding and the mutual agreement procedure with respect to a case shall terminate. Clause (i) provides that the arbitration proceeding and the mutual agreement procedure with respect to a case shall terminate if the competent authorities of the Contracting States reach a mutual agreement to resolve the case. Clause (ii) provides that the arbitration proceeding and the mutual agreement procedure with respect to a case shall terminate if the presenter of the case withdraws the request for arbitration, as is the case for the mutual agreement procedure as a general matter. Clause (iii) provides that the arbitration proceeding and the mutual agreement procedure with respect to a case shall terminate if any concerned person, or any of their representatives or agents, willfully violates the written statement of nondisclosure referred to in clause (iii) of subparagraph (c) of paragraph 6, and the competent authorities of both Contracting States agree that such violation should result in the termination of the arbitration proceeding. Finally, clause (iv) provides that the arbitration proceeding and the mutual agreement procedure with respect to a case shall terminate if any concerned person initiates a legal action or suit before the courts of either Contracting State concerning any issue involved in the case, unless such legal action or suit is suspended according to the applicable laws of the Contracting State.

New subparagraph 21(c) of the Protocol to 1990 sets forth the rule governing the submission of proposed resolutions for consideration by the arbitration panel. The competent authority of each of the Contracting States shall be permitted to submit a proposed resolution addressing each adjustment or similar issue raised in the case. Such proposed resolution shall be a resolution of the entire case and shall reflect without modification all matters in the case previously agreed between the competent authorities of both of the Contracting States. Such proposed resolution shall be limited to a disposition of specific monetary amounts (for example, of income, profit, gain or expense) or, where specified, the maximum rate of tax charged pursuant to the

Convention for each adjustment or similar issue in the case. The competent authority of each of the Contracting States shall also be permitted to submit a supporting position paper for consideration by the arbitration panel.

New subparagraph 21(d) of the Protocol of 1990 provides a special rule for proposed resolutions involving an initial determination of a threshold question (such as the existence of a permanent establishment). Subparagraph 21(d) provides that notwithstanding the provisions of subparagraph 21(c), it is understood that, in the case of an arbitration proceeding concerning: i) the tax liability of an individual with respect to whose State of residence the competent authorities have been unable to reach agreement; ii) the taxation of the business profits of an enterprise with respect to which the competent authorities have been unable to reach an agreement on whether a permanent establishment exists; or iii) such other issues the determination of which are contingent on resolution of similar threshold questions, the proposed resolutions and position papers may include positions regarding the relevant threshold questions in clause i), ii) or iii) above (for example, the question of whether a permanent establishment exists), in addition to proposed resolutions to the contingent determinations (for example, the determination of the amount of profit attributable to such permanent establishment). The determination of the arbitration panel regarding the initial threshold question may preclude the need for a further determination regarding contingent determinations.

New subparagraph 21(e) of the Protocol of 1990 provides that where an arbitration proceeding concerns a case comprising multiple adjustments or issues each requiring a disposition of specific monetary amounts of income, profit, gain or expense or, where specified, the maximum rate of tax charged pursuant to the Convention, the proposed resolution may propose a separate disposition for each adjustment or similar issue. This flexibility permits each adjustment or issue to be resolved independently through the arbitration proceeding, such that the determination of the arbitration panel will constitute a mutual agreement of the entirety of the issues in the case.

New subparagraph 21(f) of the Protocol of 1990 provides that each of the competent authorities of the Contracting States shall receive the proposed resolution and position paper submitted by the other competent authority, and shall be permitted to submit a reply submission to the arbitration panel. Each of the competent authorities of the Contracting States shall also receive the reply submission of the other competent authority.

New subparagraph 21(g) of the Protocol of 1990 provides that the presenter of the case shall be permitted to submit for consideration by the arbitration panel a paper setting forth the presenter's analysis and views of the case. The submission by the presenter of the case is not a proposed resolution that the arbitration panel could select in making its determination. The submission by the presenter may not include any information not previously provided to the competent authorities prior to the initiation of an arbitration proceeding. The competent authorities should determine an appropriate time frame for submission of such paper by the presenter in order to ensure that the competent authorities have sufficient time to consider the information.

New subparagraph 21(h) of the Protocol of 1990 provides that the arbitration panel shall deliver a determination in writing to the competent authorities of the Contracting States. The determination reached by the arbitration panel in the arbitration proceeding shall be limited to one of the proposed resolutions for the case submitted by one of the competent authorities of the Contracting States for each adjustment or similar issue and any threshold questions, and shall not include a rationale or any other explanation of the determination. The determination of the arbitration panel shall have no precedential value with respect to the application of the Convention in any other case.

New subparagraph 21(i) of the Protocol of 1990 provides that unless the competent authorities of both Contracting States agree to a longer time period, the presenter of the case shall have 45 days from receiving the determination of the arbitration panel to notify, in writing, the competent authority of the Contracting State to whom the case was presented, his acceptance of the determination. In the event the case is pending in litigation, each concerned person who is a party to the litigation must also advise, within the same time frame, the relevant court of its acceptance of the determination of the arbitration panel as the resolution by mutual agreement and its intention to withdraw from the consideration of the court the issues resolved through the proceeding. If any concerned person fails to so advise the relevant competent authority and relevant court within this time frame, the determination of the arbitration panel shall be considered not to have been accepted by the presenter of the case. Where the determination of the arbitration panel is not accepted, the case will not be eligible for any subsequent further consideration by the competent authorities.

New subparagraph 21(j) of the Protocol of 1990 provides that the fees and expenses of the members of the arbitration panel, as well as any costs incurred in connection with the proceeding by the Contracting States, shall be borne equitably by the competent authorities of Contracting States.

Article XV

This Article contains rules for bringing the Protocol into force and giving effect to its provisions.

Paragraph 1

Paragraph 1 obligates the governments of the Contracting States to notify each other through diplomatic channels when the internal procedures required by each Contracting State for the entry into force of the Protocol have been complied with. In the United States, the process leading to ratification and entry into force is as follows: Once a treaty has been signed by authorized representatives of the two Contracting States, the Department of State sends the treaty to the President who formally transmits it to the Senate for its advice and consent to ratification, which requires approval by two-thirds of the Senators present and voting. Prior to this vote, however, it generally has been the practice for the Senate Committee on Foreign Relations to hold hearings on the treaty and make a recommendation regarding its approval to the full Senate. Both Government and private sector witnesses may testify at these hearings. After the Senate gives its advice and consent to ratification of the protocol or treaty, an instrument of ratification is drafted for the President's signature. The President's signature completes the process in the United States.

Paragraph 2

Paragraph 2 provides that the Protocol will enter into force three months following the date of the later of the Notes referred to in paragraph 1. The date on which a treaty enters into force is not necessarily the date on which its provisions take effect. Paragraph 2, therefore, also contains rules that determine when the provisions of the treaty will have effect.

Under subparagraph 2(a), the Protocol will have effect with respect to taxes withheld at source (principally dividends, interest and royalties) for amounts paid or credited on or after the date on which the Protocol enters into force. For example, if the later of the Notes referred to in paragraph 1 is dated April 25 of a given year, the withholding rates specified in new Article 11 of the Convention as amended by Article V of the Protocol would be applicable to any interest paid or credited on or after July 25 of that year. This rule allows the benefits of the withholding reductions to be put into effect without waiting until the following year. The delay of three months is required to allow sufficient time for withholding agents to be informed about the change in withholding rates. If for some reason a withholding agent withholds at a higher rate than that provided by the Convention (perhaps because it was not able to re-program its computers before the payment is made), a beneficial owner of the income that is a resident of the other Contracting State may make a claim for refund pursuant to section 1464 of the Code.

Under subparagraph 2(b), the Protocol will have effect with respect to taxes determined with reference to a taxable period beginning on or after the date on which the Protocol enters into force.

For all other taxes, subparagraph 2(c) specifies that the Protocol will have effect on or after the date on which the Protocol enters into force.

Paragraph 3

Paragraph 3 sets forth additional rules regarding the applicability of the mandatory binding arbitration rules provided in paragraphs 5, 6 of revised Article 26 of the Convention as amended by Article XII of the Protocol.

Under paragraph 3, paragraphs 5 and 6 of revised Article 26 of the Convention are not effective for cases that are under consideration by the competent authorities as of the date on which the Protocol enters into force. For cases that come under such consideration after the Protocol enters into force, the provision of paragraphs 5 and 6 of revised Article 26 of the Convention shall have effect on the date on which the competent authorities agree in writing on a mode of application pursuant to subparagraph (g) of paragraph 6 of Article 26. In addition, the commencement date for cases that are under consideration by the competent authorities as of the date on or after which the Convention enters into force, but before such provisions have effect, is the date on which the competent authorities have agreed in writing on the mode of application.

Other

The various provisions in the Memorandum of Understanding are explained above in the relevant portions of the Technical Explanation with the exception of paragraph 2. Paragraph 2 provides that with reference to paragraph 3 of the Protocol of 1990, the Contracting States commit to initiate discussions as soon as possible, but no later than six months after entry into force of the Protocol, regarding the conclusion of an appropriate agreement to avoid double taxation on investments between Puerto Rico and Spain.